College-Ready

*Preparing Black and Latina/o Youth
for Higher Education—
A Culturally Relevant Approach*

College-Ready

Preparing Black and Latina/o Youth for
Higher Education—
A Culturally Relevant Approach

Michelle G. Knight
Joanne E. Marciano

Foreword by Ronald S. Rochon

Teachers College, Columbia University
New York and London

Published by Teachers College Press, 1234 Amsterdam Avenue, New York, NY 10027

Copyright © 2013 by Teachers College, Columbia University

Library of Congress Cataloging-in-Publication Data

Knight, Michelle G.

College-ready : preparing black and Latina/o youth for higher education, a culturally relevant approach / Michelle G. Knight, Joanne E. Marciano ; foreword by Ronald S. Rochon.
     pages cm
Includes bibliographical references and index.
ISBN 978-0-8077-5412-2 (pbk. : alk. paper)
ISBN 978-0-8077-5413-9 (hardcover : alk. paper)
     1. Hispanic Americans—Education (Secondary) 2. African Americans—Education (Secondary) 3. High school graduates—United States. 4. College attendance—United States. I. Marciano, Joanne E. II. Title.
LC2779.K55   2013
373.180973—dc23   2012047518

ISBN 978-0-8077-5412-2 (paper)
ISBN 978-0-8077-5413-9 (hardcover)

Printed on acid-free paper
Manufactured in the United States of America

20   19   18   17   16   15   14   13   8   7   6   5   4   3   2   1

Dedication

To the youth and their families who shared their lives with us to support the college aspirations and goals of future generations

Contents

Foreword

We Real Cool

The Pool Players.
Seven at the Golden Shovel.

We real cool. We
Left school. We

Lurk late. We
Strike straight. We

Sing sin. We
Thin gin. We

Jazz June. We
Die soon.

—Gwendolyn Brooks (1959)

When one reads the poem "We Real Cool" by Gwendolyn Brooks it is hard to imagine that community members, law enforcement officers, legislators, or even teachers would identify the pool players she speaks of as college bound or college-ready. When one considers what Americans have been taught about the contemporary urban "pool players," far too often, our minds automatically form a set of worrisome images and phrases: Black, Latina/o, dropout, ill-prepared, undocumented, violent, incarcerated, tardy, expelled, special education, angry, fatherless, and early death (just to name a few).

Ms. Brooks provides a visual image from 1959 that mirrors the reality faced today by too many Black and Brown children. In fact, for a majority of urban and rural under-served communities across the United States, "we left school, . . . we die soon" has in fact become a sad and pervasive reality. Further, for an ever-increasing number of our nation's children, that is their perceived and only option. The bloodshed which the world read about last summer in Chicago is just one of many examples of this reality. Such communities as these, all across America, are in a vicious and perpetual cycle of poverty with slim opportunities. In order to break this cycle, we need revolutionary thinking (not new testing), more compassion (not more control), and more trust (not more supervision).

In this regard, Knight and Marciano's work is pivotal. *College-Ready* brings courage and a bold urgency to the discussion of college readiness for children who have been written off by too many educators, administrators, and in some cases their own parents. By extension, these children have internalized failure and have imposed it upon themselves. *College-Ready* provides an analysis of pre-college experiences that open up new pathways for discussing and exploring what it means for African American and Latina/o students to become college-ready. The authors highlight a non-negotiable and unwavering approach toward higher education policy that places an emphasis on recognizing and building upon the strengths students bring to their educational experiences. When reading their narrative, one cannot help but hear a clear and uplifting call for both PreK–12 teachers and college educators to do better, to do right, and to work harder at finding ways to facilitate culturally relevant and responsive educational experiences for "all" students.

We are in a new century, but educational approaches directed or aimed toward our children have not advanced much. It's not 1959 anymore, but we are still presented with a barrage of negative constructs pertaining to Black and Brown children. The reality of a high school dropout rate exceeding 50% for both groups in many school districts across the United States, and moreover, our educational policy responses to these realities, seem tired and bland at best. For example, we are overwhelmingly focused on issues such as parent involvement, which is often interpreted as moving the total responsibility for student success from the schools to the shoulders of parents. We must remember that parents are not trained educators. This seems comical at best and cruel at worst, when applied to under-served communities. In such communities parents received the same inadequate educational experiences and resources their children are now receiving. The cycle appears again. Yet, policymakers who promote parent/guardian/family engagement ask parents, who have been failed by their own schools, to somehow take up the slack for their children's schools by providing external educational support and resources that they do not possess.

We are in a crippling downturn. Thankfully scholars like Michelle Knight and Joanne Marciano provide us with the courage to ask critical questions. Questions such as, "How do we develop genuine and trusting relationships between families and school administrators?" And, more importantly, "How can schools build long-term trusting relationships with children?" For they, too, one day may become parents.

Professor Knight and Ms. Marciano have a chapter in their book titled, "Creating a Culturally Relevant School-wide College-going Culture." The point of this chapter is to challenge inadequate national and state policies and assumptions that are so weak or misguided that they seem to reinforce the idea that some children (based on race, gender, language, or zip code) need not be given the opportunity to go to college. In response, these researchers' findings encourage us to work to empower all children with opportunities to develop their own voices. And, perhaps most important, educators, administrators, and policymakers are encouraged to provide space in the policy debate and in the educational process to allow parents and students to have serious input into curriculum development.

In closing, I urge all who are concerned about the educational well-being of both Latina/o and African American youth to read this book. Knight and Marciano have poured their hearts into this effort, identifying critical areas of concerns facing student success. They also comment on the often-overlooked resources within both school and community. Note, they do not provide us with a "recipe" or "magic bullet" as an answer to this national crisis. They brilliantly push the reader to do something different, bold, creative, and innovative. These two scholars have charged us to engage family and community with authentic and sincere methods of inclusion, while demanding that we respect all who are engaged in the educational process, especially parents and children. They refuse to accept leaving school, jazzing June, and most importantly, "we die soon."

—Ronald S. Rochon, PhD,
Provost, University of Southern Indiana

Acknowledgments

Michelle G. Knight: This book is a collective endeavor supported by family, mentors, graduate students, and women of color throughout history whose courage serves as a beacon to continue to challenge educational injustices. My sister Amy has been there with me every step of the way and has provided immeasurable love, support, and encouragement. I am also thankful for the unique encouraging relationships with my brothers: Bill's silent yet strong backing, Richard's greatest compliment in saying that he hoped his girls would "be" in the world as I am, Michael's love which knows no bounds. Then there is my mother's belief that I could do anything and my father who instilled in his children that a "good" education meant the ability to thrive in ways that might not have been afforded to him as a Black young man. Mentors and friends in the academy, Celia Genishi, Ronald Rochon, Sylvia Celedon-Pattichis, and Heather Oesterreich, continuously inspire me to reach new heights in my professional and personal life.

I would also like to thank the institutions and people who made the research study possible. I am thankful for the generous support of the Spencer Foundation through the National Academy of Education Postdoctoral Fellowship Program and the Small Research Grants Program. There are also many graduate students who contributed immensely to the research reported in this book and without whom the work could not have been completed. I would also like to extend our thanks to the editorial members of Teachers College Press who have supported the book's preparation and whose insights helped us throughout the process. Finally, I am enormously grateful to all the students in the middle and high schools whom I have had the honor to teach and to conduct research with, and whose spirit challenges me to keep working on behalf of all children and youth.

Joanne E. Marciano: Throughout this work, I have been guided and supported by many. My parents, Samuel and Mary Marciano; my family, Vaughn W. M. Watson, Carmela F. M. Watson, and Carter F. M. Watson; my siblings, Diana Brach, Tim Marciano, Laura Marciano, and their families; my friends of more than 20 years, Alisa O'Brien, Julie Mungo, Kristen Siewert, Marla Waiss, and Michelle Franzone; and my extended family, including Marion and Koach Coleman, and Nicole Gesualdo graciously share their love and encouragement. I am also extremely thankful to Michelle G. Knight whose generosity and mentorship challenge and inspire me to seek out possibility; and to Sonja Cherry-Paul, Dana Johansen, Tara Lencl, Paula Holmes, and the many educators I am fortunate to work with and learn from. Finally, I thank the youth with whom I have had the privilege to work for sharing so generously of their experiences and their insights.

CHAPTER 1

Introduction

Creating a Culturally Relevant, Schoolwide, College-Going Culture

I know that for me to understand college I have to be shown and guided by people older than me or who have the knowledge of what is required to go to college.

—Amena, Black, female student

This is high school, and if you're not teaching your kids so that they can get into college and go on with what they're doing, I don't know what you're doing in a high school; because we're no longer in a society that takes a high school diploma as enough, it's not enough anymore.

—Ms. Smith, White, music teacher

I think the idea of wanting something better for themselves in the future than what they have right now. I think there's much more of an impetus for the kids in our school than there was for, let's say, me, in my school. I was in a middle to upper middle class suburb in northern Westchester. And it was like a given. So you go to college, you know. No big deal. But I think they have much more of an incentive. They're much more hungry. . . . Because they want something they don't have.

—Ms. Martin, White, guidance counselor

In the quotations above, Amena, Ms. Smith, and Ms. Martin invite us into their conversations, highlighting the ways working class Black and Latina/o urban youth and their predominantly White teachers, administrators, and counselors understand and negotiate college-going processes at a New York City public high school. They speak candidly as they challenge and move away from traditional deficit views of Black and Latina/o youth as not caring about their education, positioning them instead as college bound with desires for a better future. At the same time, they raise issues of the importance of college readiness and access for youth; questions about the ways social class, race, and ethnicity matter in meeting youth's educational needs, and how teachers, counselors, and administrators may support them in preparing for college. Significantly, their voices bring to light the complexities of the individual and collective lives of students, teachers, counselors, administrators, and families as they are experienced in the midst of increased student diversity and educational inequity in schools throughout the United States. In fact, public schools in the 21st century serve an unprecedented, increasingly diverse population of 49 million students who come to school with multiple racial, cultural, linguistic, family, and economic backgrounds. Students bring multiple experiences, multiple levels of familiarity with the demands of school, and multiple strengths. Problematic is the understanding that while there are more students of color in schools than ever before, the high school graduation rates of White and Asian students are at 78.8% and 80%, respectively. The graduation rates of Black and Latina/o youth, meanwhile, hover around 50%, with even fewer going on to attend college (Editorial Projects in Education, 2012; U.S. Department of Education, 2009). Clearly, the educational preparation of working class Black and Latina/o students for high school graduation, college readiness, and access needs to change.

Further complicating issues of college readiness for working class Black and Latina/o youth across the United States is the traditional model for college access for 11th- and 12th-graders, and the tendency of students, their families, and school communities to emphasize the role of guidance counselors as the primary sources of information about college (Hossler & Gallagher, 1987; McDonough, 1997; Perna, Rowan-Kenyon, Thomas, Anderson, & Li, 2008). In private schools students often have access to comprehensive college counseling structures (McDonough, 1997). However, high student to counselor ratios in low-resource schools typically serving Black and Latina/o students, which can reach as high as 740:1, make it difficult for counselors to effectively provide information about college to all students (Farmer-Hinton & McCullough, 2008). Perhaps even more compelling is evidence from a recent study of high school graduates who said that their guidance counselors did not provide them with as much useful information about college as normative conceptions of guidance counselors might lead us to believe (Steinberg, 2010). Rather, it was students' teachers who provided the most useful insight into students' futures. Therefore, while guidance counselors remain important and influential school staff members in the college-going process, we contend that a shift in the preparation of college readiness and access is needed. Teachers, counselors, and administrators can partner together to ensure more effective college readiness and access to a range of college institutions by creating a culturally relevant, schoolwide, college-going culture for all students across 9th–12th grades. For, as Ms. Smith points out in the opening of this chapter, all those working within secondary schools are charged with preparing today's youth for access to college.

In *College-Ready*, we focus on the voices, perspectives, and actions of 25 working class Black and Latina/o students and interviews with more than 50 of their teachers, counselors, administrators, and families to better understand who and what influences youth's college-going processes. We seek to provide high school teachers, counselors, and administrators insight into ways that they can partner together to create a culturally relevant, schoolwide, college-going culture to increase Black and Latina/o youth's access to college. Such a schoolwide culture recognizes the importance of including students' cultural backgrounds and references in all aspects of learning (Ladson-Billings, 1994a), particularly as related to preparing for, applying to, and enrolling in college, or what we refer to throughout this text as engaging in college-going processes. Teachers', counselors', and administrators' doing so is especially important across the 9th–12th-grade levels due to the current context of increased student diversity within schools, existing national and state educational policies and practices aimed at preparing students for college access, and the urgency of research demonstrating that successful preparation for college access begins long before 11th and 12th grades.

This chapter explores the sociocultural, historical, and political context in which teachers, counselors, and administrators are working to prepare Black and Latina/o youth for a range of postsecondary institutions. Taken together, the contexts of increasing demographic diversity and educational achievement status of Black and Latina/o youth, in addition to national and state-level policies enacted in high schools, and culturally relevant teaching practices enable a more current, complex, and nuanced understanding of college readiness and access. We then provide a brief overview of the study that addresses how students' and their teachers', counselors', administrators', and families' meanings and understandings of college-going processes influence students' college readiness and access. As you read further about the current context within which educational policies and practices about college readiness and access exist, we ask you to critically reflect on the ways in which you are situated within this changing context and what supports or hinders your success in preparing working class Black and Latina/o youth for college.

THE DEMOGRAPHIC IMPERATIVE

We have a great diversity of students at Evergreen just like at any other
high school in New York City. We're not unique. The majority of our students
are Latino and African American and we have a small group of Asians and I
don't know if we have White kids. I've seen White kids, but I'm not sure that
they're really White. If you know what I mean. Some Hispanic kids could be
very White and you don't know. Although I do have one Polish student. So I
don't know, 1–2 percent of our kids are White? We have students who come
from different social and economic backgrounds and the majority are poor
families, parents not educated beyond high school.

—Ms. Estevez, Latina, guidance counselor

And the thing is, most of my teachers were White. I had very few teachers
who were Black. It's either White or Hispanic. That's it. . . . I started
thinking, and in this school, I've maybe seen five Black teachers? And this is
a huge school. We have, what, two hundred teachers I think here? Or three
hundred?

—Mr. Cortez, Latino, art teacher

Indeed, the demographic diversity within this school is not unique to New
York, and issues of college readiness and access for Black and Latina/o youth
are significant to students, administrators, teachers, and counselors in communities across the nation. Black and Latina/o students now constitute the
majority of students in many of the major urban school districts in the country. Although no two schools or communities are exactly alike, students of
color make up more than 50% of the children in the largest school districts
in the United States, which include, but are not limited to, New York, Los
Angeles, Las Vegas, San Diego, Miami, Houston, and Philadelphia (Sleeter,
2005). Additionally, their increasing presence in many of the surrounding
suburbs draws attention to the "new" reality that teachers in both urban
and suburban areas are teaching children of color, who, in many instances,
include a growing presence of Latina/o students (Buendia, 2010). Significantly, a recent study of the 4 million children in the Kindergarten class of
2010–2011 reveals that nearly 25% of 5-year-olds in the United States are
Hispanic and that nearly 22% of 5-year-olds do not speak English at home
(El Nassar & Overberg, 2010).

While the population of students of color increased steadily from 35.1%
to 42.8% during the 10-year span from 1995 to 2005 (U.S. Department of

Education, 2009), the consistently stable demographic profile of teachers has drawn considerable attention to issues of diversity and equity in the literature on teacher preparation and the teaching of diverse student populations. Public school teachers are 84% White, 7.8% African American, 5.7% Hispanic, 1.6% Asian American, and 0.8% Native American (U.S. Department of Education, 2009). Further complicating the picture is that the majority of pre-service teachers entering the field are female, White, monolingual, middle class, and from small towns and rural areas (Cochran-Smith, Davis, & Fries, 2003; Hollins & Torres Guzman, 2005; Zumwalt & Craig, 2005). Of teachers entering the field, Whites constitute 80.5%, African Americans 9%, Hispanics 4.7%, Asian and Pacific Americans 1.7%, and Native Americans 1.7% (Zumwalt & Craig, 2005). These demographics contribute to policy questions surrounding the skills, knowledge, and dispositions or cultural competencies needed in the preparation of all teachers for diverse student populations in the midst of debates on how teachers teach and work with diverse student populations and what constitutes culturally relevant teaching and educational equity.

The urgency for all teachers, counselors, and administrators to enact culturally relevant educational policies and practices that provide all of their students with opportunities to successfully negotiate school contexts in order to excel academically and prepare for and enroll in college is intensified in light of the current crisis in educational achievement levels of working class Black and Latina/o youth. To create a culturally relevant, schoolwide, college-going culture, it is important to examine current educational achievement levels, recent national policies such as the development of the Common Core Standards for College Readiness and Access, high school policies and programs relating to college access such as the AVID program, and culturally relevant pedagogical practices that support students' educational opportunities for success. In bringing these contexts together, teachers, counselors, and administrators can better understand the national disparities in educational opportunities and thus far what has facilitated or hindered Black and Latina/o youth's school experiences and access to college.

EDUCATIONAL ACHIEVEMENT

Many of today's educators are well aware that access to higher education has long been seen as a stepping stone to increased job opportunities, higher salaries, and quality of life benefits. Current economic conditions, in which significant levels of unemployment are leading to higher levels of competition among job seekers, bring an increased sense of urgency to discussions of college readiness and access, particularly for youth from working class Black and Latina/o backgrounds. Whereas the current economic climate has challenged those holding a college degree to obtain a job, the economic outlook for those without a college degree is even bleaker. As Bedolla (2010) found in her review of research on postsecondary transitions, a college credential is crucial for attaining a high paying job in the U.S. economy of the 21st century. Additionally, a college education affords numerous individual and societal benefits, such as increased leadership in communities and voting patterns (Gándara, 2002), that should not be underestimated or ignored. For example, youth who attend college are more likely than those who do not to engage in civic learning and action, according to Flanagan, Levine, and Settersten (2011), who found that college educated youth held higher levels of civic engagement than youth who had not attended college.

Despite the importance and benefits of attaining a college degree, vast discrepancies exist in educational outcomes among students. Discussions of these inequities often focus on the well-known and persistent achievement gap in test scores that separates our nation's Black and Latina/o students from their higher performing White and Asian peers in critical subjects. These inequitable outcomes, however, go far beyond test scores and show up as well in a host of other indicators of achievement, including dropout rates, high school graduation rates, college attendance and completion, and job attainment. In fact, research on educational equity reveals the inequities of attainment and access by varied populations at all levels of schooling, from elementary to postsecondary. For example, a recent study by the Editorial Projects in Education Research Center (2012) found that at the national level, 73.4% of students graduated from high school in 2009. While such statistics are troubling in themselves, considerations of graduation rates by racial/ethnic group provide further cause for concern. In fact, 78.8% of White students and 80.5% of Asian students graduated from high school in that year, yet only 63.3% of Hispanic students and 58.7% of Black students earned high school diplomas (we utilize the descriptor "Hispanic" when citing sources that do so, including census data and government reports). Even those numbers may not accurately depict the percentages of students who leave high school before graduating. An even more disturbing picture reveals further disparities across race/ethnicity and gender. Hispanic and Black females are graduating at 66.1% and 65.3%, respectively, while Hispanic and Black males are graduating at the much lower rates of 58.1% and 51.9%, respectively (Editorial Projects in Education Research Center, 2012). A similar story plays out at the state level. For example, a recent report on the graduating class of 2009 in New Mexico demonstrates that only about 62.3% of Hispanic students and 35.8% of Black students are attaining a high school diploma (Editorial Projects in Education Research

Center, 2012). These statistics are particularly troubling considering the large percentage of Latina/os living in New Mexico. According to 2010 census figures, more than 46% of the population in New Mexico is of Hispanic or Latino origin (U.S. Census Bureau, 2010). In the states of New York and California, the numbers are even bleaker. Only about 57.6% of Black students and 57.9% of Hispanic students graduate from high school in New York State, while 50.8% of Black students and 63% of Hispanic students in California graduate (Editorial Projects in Education Research Center, 2012).

Considering the graduation rates described above, it is not surprising that Black and Latina/o youth are not entering college or earning college degrees at equitable rates relative to White students at both the national and state levels (Choy, Horn, Nunez, & Chen, 2000; Gándara & Contreras, 2009). In 2007, for example, only 11% of American college students were Latina/o, while 13% were Black (U.S. Department of Education, 2009). Recent trends also have highlighted that more women than men are attending college, with females making up 57% of students enrolled in Title IV degree-granting institutions in the United States and males constituting 43% of students (U.S. Department of Education, 2009). Black males and Latinos are earning degrees at rates far below those of White students and Black females and Latinas (Sleeter & Grant, 2009).

These disparities reflect the reality that many minority and poor students encounter markedly inadequate educational opportunities in their K–12 education (Gibson, Gándara, & Koyama, 2004), and debates abound about how to best address them. The importance of acting upon these educational disparities and educating working class Black and Latina/o students within the United States is paramount in improving their high school educational experiences and bridging their transition from K–12 schools to postsecondary options. Recent efforts to address these inequitable educational opportunities have focused on national and state policies enacted to improve educational opportunities and college readiness and access for working class Black and Latina/o youth.

NATIONAL AND STATE POLICIES: COLLEGE READINESS AND ACCESS

Toward the goal of increasing college access and college readiness among youth in the United States, national, state, and local policies have drawn upon decades of research to recommend a variety of policies and practices. Most recently, at the national level, a focus on curriculum is being forefronted in the quest to prepare students for academic success in college. A total of

45 states across the nation have adopted a set of Common Core Standards, developed by the National Governors Association Center for Best Practices, aimed at preparing students "for success in college and careers" (Common Core State Standards, 2011). As states competed for more than $3.4 billion in federal Race to the Top financing to develop programs and policies aimed at realizing the goal of increasing college access and readiness set forth by the Common Core Standards (Dylan, 2010), preparing today's students to be competitive in an increasingly global marketplace continued to remain at the forefront of debates about the quality of education in the United States.

While the focus on increasing academic rigor and student performance in key areas such as literacy and math is a laudable goal of the Common Core State Standards Initiative, we argue that the standards in themselves do not necessarily increase youth's understanding of how to engage in college-going processes. For example, to be successful in college, youth certainly need to demonstrate the ability to succeed academically in a college-level curriculum. Yet students who do not have access to information about how to apply to college, or how to choose a college that will best serve their interests and needs, will not learn those things solely by engaging in a rigorous college preparatory curriculum. Unfortunately, research has shown that low-income youth typically have less access to information about applying to college than their upper and middle class peers. A lack of information about preparing for and enrolling in college prevents many low-income students from achieving their college-going aspirations. For example, Kirst and Venezia (2004) found that students who did not have access to information about college incorrectly assumed that they couldn't afford college, that they had to be a stellar athlete or student to receive financial aid, and that meeting high school graduation requirements would prepare them to enroll in college.

Rather than continue to position teachers as singularly responsible for enacting curriculum within their classrooms, we argue that teachers are among broader ranks of school personnel who have the opportunity to support students' engagement in all aspects of applying to college, not just in their academic preparation. Although some teachers may express discomfort with sharing information about college due to their own perceived lack of information about college-going processes (Kirst & Venezia, 2004), opportunities exist for teachers to directly support youth's access to college. Through discussions with youth about their own experiences navigating the various components of the college application process, their voiced expectations that youth attend college, and their facilitation of visits to college campuses, teachers may partner with students to engage in a rigorous curriculum that supports youth in actually applying to college, not just preparing academically to attend. While the development of the Common Core Standards has drawn increased attention to working class

Black and Latina/o students' preparation for, application to, and enrollment in college, state- and local-level policies have focused on additional factors beyond academic preparation that support youth in enrolling in college. For first-generation college applicants, students of color, and/or low-income students, engagement in a culturally relevant college preparatory program supportive of youth's cultural, social, and academic development has shown promise for increasing youth's access to college. We argue that such programs, which typically focus on small cohorts of students attending a school, have the potential to be expanded schoolwide, creating access to college for larger numbers of students.

HIGH SCHOOL POLICIES AND PRACTICES

Like many educators, researchers, and policymakers, we believe that schools remain sites of possibility when it comes to increasing access to college. A number of college preparatory programs implemented within schools attended by Black and Latina/o youth have very successfully provided students with access to college. Programs such as Advancement Via Individual Determination (AVID), Puente, Gaining Early Awareness and Readiness for Undergraduate Programs (GEAR UP), Upward Bound, and the Liberty Partnerships Program (LPP) provide opportunities for Black and Latina/o youth to engage in school-based activities aimed at increasing college readiness by building upon youth's cultural backgrounds and facilitating their development of supportive peer groups (Hubbard & Mehan, 1999; Knight & Oesterreich, 2002; Loza, 2003; Moreno, 2002; Watt, Huerta, & Lozana, 2007; Watt, Powell, & Mendiola, 2004). In many instances, the programs are successful in supporting the academic achievement and scores on college admissions exams, such as the PSAT and SAT, of the youth who participate (Watt, Powell, & Mendiola, 2004).

At the state level, programs also have been implemented toward the goal of increasing youth's access to college. In New York State, for example, the LPP was developed to provide schooling opportunities for "at risk" students to graduate from high school and be prepared to enter postsecondary education or the workforce. In their examination of two LPP sites, Knight and Oesterreich (2002) argue for the importance of attending to youth's multiple intersecting identities of race, class, and gender within their local contexts to improve their educational experiences and access to college. For example, those authors argue for understanding the identities and cultures of Black and Latina/o adolescents in their local context in order to build on the strengths of their families and communities to provide services that will meet their needs. Simply focusing on curriculum, while a necessary component of increasing college access, is not enough to meet the multifaceted needs of youth.

Access even to the college preparatory programs described above, however, remains out of reach for many Black and Latina/o students. For example, in a review of research literature focused on the college preparation programs AVID, Upward Bound, and the University of California's Early Academic Outreach Program, Loza (2003) found that the stringent eligibility requirements of most college preparatory programs, related to aspects of a student's educational profile, including academic history, prevent many students who would benefit from participation from doing so. Additionally, schoolwide tracking policies often position students as belonging to honors, general, or remedial courses based on their standardized testing performance (Oakes, Rogers, Lipton, & Morrell, 2002). These tracking procedures typically result in honors students' access to the most rigorous level of coursework, leaving students not labeled honors, particularly those in remedial education tracks, with limited avenues for pursuing the rigorous coursework needed to support their college readiness and access. In consideration of these findings, we argue for the development of a culturally relevant, schoolwide, college-going culture so that all students are prepared for college, rather than just individual students selected to participate in what Gándara (2002) refers to as student-centered programs.

The call for school-centered change is echoed by more recent research focusing on the necessary dimensions of creating a culture of college going in high school. Corwin and Tierney (2007) argue that, in general, a college culture in high school "cultivates aspirations and behaviors conducive to preparing for, applying to, and enrolling in college" (p. 3). They argue that a college culture is inclusive and accessible to all students through five key factors:

1. academic momentum that supports a rigorous academic curriculum;
2. an understanding of how college plans are developed from youth's future aspirations;
3. a clear mission statement based on the school's expectations for all of its students to attend college;
4. comprehensive college services that provide guidance, preparation, and information about the college process; and
5. coordinated and systemic college supports for youth in which all stakeholders, such as students, families, high school personnel—administrators, teachers, counselors—and college partnerships personnel engage together to develop and actualize college goals for students.

More specifically, in creating a schoolwide culture of college going, McClafferty, McDonough, and Nunez (2002) argue that one solitary professional, such as a college counselor or advisor, is not solely responsible for facilitating college access for all students. Rather, all educators within the school would engage in "college talk," explicit conversation with students about what it takes to get to college; clear expectations that all students can go to college; a comprehensive counseling model, testing, and curriculum coursework aligned to ensure students' academic success; and the involvement of school faculty, parents, and college personnel.

In moving away from the traditional model of college readiness and access focused primarily on 11th- and 12th-graders and enacted by counselors, we further extend the research described above to illuminate how a framework of culturally relevant, schoolwide, college-going policies and practices for teachers, counselors, and administrators may begin to position Black and Latina/o youth as "successful negotiators" of school contexts while increasing their college readiness and access. This framework, in part, has been situated as an educational reform effort based on Gloria Ladson-Billings's tenets of culturally relevant teaching (Ladson-Billings, 1994a, 1995, 2001), a promising pedagogical approach positioned to best meet the educational and social needs of culturally and linguistically diverse students and to change the educational inequities and deficit views many working class Black and Latina/o youth face every day (Dutro, Kazemi, Balf, & Yin-Sheue, 2008; Howard, 2001; Ladson-Billings, 1995, 2001). By including a culturally relevant education framework, we highlight the ways in which the tenets of culturally relevant teaching can inform the educational policies and practices needed in a schoolwide college-going culture to better prepare working class Black and Latina/o youth to be college-ready and pursue a college education.

CULTURALLY RELEVANT EDUCATORS, POLICIES, AND PRACTICES FOR COLLEGE ACCESS

Gloria Ladson-Billings (1994a, 2001) describes three tenets, or outcomes for students, of culturally relevant teaching. These include academic achievement, cultural competence, and sociopolitical consciousness. First, culturally relevant teachers clearly explain what achievement means in their particular classroom and the ways students can obtain it through a variety of measures, especially as they believe all students are capable of learning and achieving academic success. Moreover, culturally relevant teachers know their subject matter, their students, and how to teach the subject matter to a particular group of students. Second, culturally relevant teachers support the cultural competence of their students. This is accomplished when teachers understand the role of culture and its function in education, their students' lives, and their own professional lives. In so doing, teachers do not seek to separate students from their home cultures. Rather, teachers use the students' culture to affirm their cultural backgrounds, build on knowledge they already possess to support them in learning new concepts and ideas, and support their college-going identities. Third, culturally relevant teachers support the sociopolitical consciousness of their students, so that students are able to develop a critical stance toward inequities in their schools, communities, and the larger society. For example, culturally relevant educators' policies and practices assist students to achieve academically, to build on and strengthen their cultural identities, and to understand, question, and critique their educational experiences. These three outcomes—academic achievement, cultural competence, and sociopolitical consciousness—may be reached in a variety of ways and are shaped by teachers', guidance counselors', and administrators' conceptions of self and others in relation to academic expectations of students, social relations, and the building of a community of learners with authentically caring relationships between and among the teacher and students' peers, and by beliefs about knowledge that can be socially constructed, viewed critically, and assessed through a variety of means (Ladson-Billings, 1995). Therefore, in the midst of dismal high school graduation rates and college acceptance rates, we are concerned with how culturally relevant teachers', counselors', and administrators' policies and practices can prepare working class Black and Latina/o students to be academically successful, culturally competent, and critically conscious to support their college readiness and access.

Academic Achievement

Culturally relevant educators, teachers, counselors, and administrators focus on students' academic achievement as one of their primary tasks and are clear with college-bound working class Black and Latina/o youth about what it means to be academically successful in their schools. Indicators of academic achievement for college-bound Black and Latina/o youth are not measured solely by standardized test scores in subject matter courses, but also by high school graduation rates and college acceptance rates. Therefore, culturally relevant educators demonstrate their professional commitment to the academic achievement of working class Black and Latina/o youth through a belief and understanding that all students can be academically successful and go to college. Scholars working to improve college access for working class Black and Latina/o youth unquestionably agree that all students need preparation for and access to a rigorous high school curriculum and college admissions exams that align with college preparation for a range of postsecondary institutions (Knight, 2003, 2010; McDonough, 1997; Tierney, Corwin, & Colyar, 2005). The Common Core Standards are working toward improving this for Black and Latina/o students by providing standards for all students to achieve, in the hopes of eliminating inequities in curricular areas of English and mathematics (Common Core State Standards, 2011). We extend this idea to say that high expectations are a part of this—not just expectations that youth will complete class assignments, but that they need access to a rigorous curriculum and assistance in being successful with it, because they are perceived as college bound. Specifically, youth need access to college preparatory courses that often exceed those that are required for their graduation from high school. In New York State, for example, general education students are required to pass five state exit exams with a grade of 65% or higher in order to graduate from high school. However, scoring 65% on such an exam does not qualify as college-ready according to indicators utilized by college admissions officers. Further, to be considered competitive at many institutions of higher education, applicants need access to courses beyond those required for high school graduation, such as Advanced Placement courses in a variety of subject areas.

In addition to a rigorous curriculum, early awareness of and preparation for standardized tests such as the SAT are critical components of supporting youth's access to college (Knight, 2010). This expectation of Black and Latina/o youth as college bound is consistently communicated to students, through school policies and practices such as "college talk" (McClafferty, McDonough, & Nunez, 2002) in which teachers, counselors, and administrators partner together to prepare students for college readiness and access to a range of postsecondary institutions. Clearly, it is important for students to develop an understanding of college requirements across a range of postsecondary institutions, including 2-year, 4-year, art-based, and performance-based colleges, and the academic knowledge needed to fulfill them. However, for many students of color, low-income students, and students who will be the first in their family to attend college, a focus on academic achievement is necessary, but not enough. These youth also will need to know how to negotiate schoolwide policies and practices that support (or not) their own cultural identities as college bound. Therefore, in addition to addressing student achievement, culturally relevant educators also help students to develop cultural competence.

Cultural Competence

Culturally relevant teachers, counselors, and administrators, regardless of whether their race/ethnicity or cultural backgrounds match those of their students, exhibit a willingness to learn about the students' cultures and communities and their ideas about college going. In so doing, they use students' cultural knowledge, cultural needs, and cultural assets as a basis for their learning, development of their multicultural college-going identities, and preparation for college readiness and access (Knight, 2010; Knight

& Oesterreich, 2002; Oakes, Rogers, Lipton, & Morrell, 2002; Villalpando & Solorzano, 2004). By multicultural college-going identities, we mean students' negotiations of college-going processes "without sacrificing one's own identity and connections with one's home community" (Oakes, Rogers, Lipton, & Morrell, 2002, p. 109). Equally important, culturally relevant educators take responsibility for understanding their own cultures, norms, and values about education and college preparation, and the ways they may facilitate or hinder students' views of themselves as college bound, their college-going cultural identities, and the college choices they make. Moreover, they seek to understand how the school's policies and practices incorporate the identities and cultures of the students as a bridge between what students already know about college and the knowledge or the college information they need to learn as part of their educational experiences in school and development of their cultural competencies as college-bound youth. The premise is that students already arrive in schools with cultural assets or "funds of knowledge" (Moll, Amanti, Neff, & Gonzalez, 1992) and understandings of how they make sense of the world and college access based on their own cultures and daily life experiences.

A case in point is the importance of viewing students' families as supportive of their children's college access, even if they have not attended college themselves. Families' and communities' aspirations for their children's futures should not be discounted or underestimated, especially as they have high expectations and provide strong emotional support for their children's education (Gonzalez, Stoner, & Jovel, 2003; Knight, Dixon, Norton, & Bentley, 2006). Further, Gonzalez, Jovel, and Stoner (2004) provide insight into the tensions and conflicts for Latinas whose parents were supportive of their daughters' college opportunities, but not those which would take them away from their homes and family environment. Culturally relevant educators need to be mindful about ways to address the tensions felt by Latinas and their families who want their children to go to a college close to home, or how to ease parents' apprehensions by focusing on the support of Latina/o faculty, staff, and other students if children go away to college. Family engagement is a critical aspect of supporting youth's college access (Tierney & Auerbach, 2005). Therefore, in affirming the cultural identities of working class Black and Latina/o youth, we question how culturally relevant educators build on families' cultural values of education and the aspirations they have for their children to further support youth's academic achievement, cultural competence, and access to college.

Sociopolitical Consciousness

The goal of creating a schoolwide college-going culture necessitates an emphasis on the culture of the student and on the development of academic skills for achievement. Equally important for culturally relevant educators is an awareness of the larger sociopolitical context of the ways in which schools, communities, the nation, and the world play a role in the educational experiences and opportunities afforded (or not) to working class Black and Latina/o youth in the United States (Ladson-Billings, 2002) and, in this case, their preparation and access to college. In seeking to understand the larger sociopolitical context of what is facilitating or hindering Black and Latina/o youth's preparation, readiness, and access for college, it is essential to understand the current statistical data on high school graduation and college attendance rates of these youth and their interactions with educational institutions. Moreover, as part of understanding the larger sociopolitical context of college access, culturally relevant educators understand the multiple challenges of preparing for, applying to, and enrolling in college that students of color, low-income students, and first-generation college goers encounter that are different from those of their wealthier White counterparts (Datnow, Solorzano, Watford, & Park, 2010; Farmer-Hinton & McCollough, 2008; McDonough, 1997; Oakes, Rogers, Lipton, & Morrell, 2002). Tierney (2009) argues that

> a great deal of preparation takes place that enables middle and upper class students to apply for college. In upper income schools the starts of activities that occur throughout a child's adolescence and especially during high school not only prepare the child to apply for college, but also foster discussions about college by an individual's peers and family. (p. 92)

Many college preparation researchers contend that this kind of preparation does not exist for those who are poor and lack supportive structures that prepare them to go to college, in the same manner as for their well-off counterparts (Datnow, Solorzano, Watford, & Park, 2010). Therefore, it is imperative that culturally relevant educators are aware of the ways in which schools facilitate or hinder youth's access to college, in order to better understand how to create a schoolwide high school college-going culture. For instance, Gonzalez, Stoner, and Jovel (2003) document the race/gender gap in achievement and how Latinas are "the least formally educated female ethnic group in the United States" (p. 147). In seeking to understand how relationships with family and school personnel affect Latina students' postsecondary options, they studied those who had who entered a 4-year college versus a community college and who had been educated in schools serving low-income students. Latinas who went to 4-year colleges had teachers who gave them access to "strong emotional support and to important information about college" (p. 160), participated in college preparation programs in their high schools, and were placed in rigorous curricular coursework that gave them access to college counselors. Moreover, recognizing that achievement is not distributed equally among ethnic groups by gender (Lopez, 2002), extracurricular activities also have come to play a dominant role in supporting males and females in the kinds of activities that engage them in school and with college preparation (Knight, 2011). Curriculum and extracurricular activities take into account and build on the ways in which race/ethnicity, gender, and class play a role in college readiness and access. In addition to curricular and extracurricular activities, culturally relevant educators engage a critical web of support from those who influence students' college-going processes, including families, mentors, and peers. For example, researchers have long engaged in understanding the role of peers and peer relations in shaping educational experiences and outcomes for students of color. They tend to document the role of peer influence as a "negative force distracting adolescents from academic engagement and achievement" (Gibson, Gándara, & Koyama, 2004, p. 174). More recently, however, researchers have begun to identify how peer influence positively impacts academic school success and college-going processes (Boudin & Knight, 2006; Tierney & Colyar, 2005). Culturally relevant educators understand the varied ways in which peer influence shapes and is shaped by the kinds of relationships students have with one another, and, in turn, how these relationships are shaped by the schools and classrooms they create. Thus, culturally relevant educators are able to view how they can foster positive peer relations among students that are not only fluid, open, and caring (Gay, 2010), but ones that allow educators to develop policies and practices that build on the role of positive peer influence in supporting youth's college-going processes.

The role that culturally relevant teachers, counselors, and administrators play in the creation of a high school college-going culture for working class Black and Latina/o youth is central to this book's goal of increasing students' access to college. We find those teachers who are engaged in culturally relevant pedagogy aimed at developing students' academic achievement, cultural competence, and sociopolitical consciousness (Ladson-Billings, 2002) to hold the most promise in moving toward the development of school communities aimed at providing access to college for all students. As educational disparities continue to exist, so, too, does the urgency and commitment of teachers, counselors, and administrators who partner together to successfully prepare youth to engage in a range of postsecondary institutions.

SCHOOL SETTING AND RESEARCH METHODS

The research study discussed throughout this book is situated at Evergreen High School (all names are pseudonyms), a New York City public school serving 3,500 poor and working class students in 9th through 12th grades, more than 90% of whom are Black and/or Latina/o; of that number 43% are male and 57% are female. Teachers at Evergreen are predominantly European American and live outside of urban communities; 85% have master's degrees or higher. Many Black and Latina/o youth and their families decided to attend Evergreen High School because of the excellent reputation of its academic and extracurricular programs. (See Appendix B for a more detailed explanation of the research context and methods.)

In an effort to make their students more aware of, prepared for, and pursuant of a variety of postsecondary institutions, this comprehensive high school utilizes smaller learning communities or "houses" to organize the student population. There are ten houses: six college or career theme houses, and four general learning houses, one for each grade. Each house has three staff personnel: a guidance counselor, a family assistant for community outreach, and a house coordinator. Moreover, the schoolwide college-going culture includes two college counselors, a learning tutorial, multiple testing subcultures, and cross-age extracurricular activities such as sports, clubs, electives, college fairs, and college visits. However, students' access to these structures varies. For example, one of the two college counselors is responsible for serving students in only one of the houses, which sends students to the most selective 4-year colleges in the United States, whereas the second college counselor serves all the students in the nine other houses. This alarming ratio of counselor to students aligns with much of the research concerning college preparation. Thus, to gain further insights into how the school could improve its college policies and practices around disparities in facilitating college preparation and access, several of the school administrators agreed to support the research study. With its increasingly diverse student population, predominantly White teaching staff, and high student to counselor ratio, Evergreen High School is reflective of the contexts of many other schools across the United States. Therefore, the overarching aim of this book is to provide high school teachers, counselors, and administrators insight into ways that they together can create culturally relevant, educational, schoolwide policies and practices that support college readiness and access for working class Black and Latina/o youth.

Toward this goal, we center the perspectives of 25 working class 9th-grade Black and Latina/o urban youth (see Table 1.1) from a 4-year ethnographic study situated at Evergreen High School in which we examined (1) who and what was influencing their college-going processes in and out of school contexts such as teachers, counselors, peers, family members, and the media (see Figure 1.1), and (2) how these youth negotiated those influences on their college-going processes.

The voices, perspectives, and actions of the youth, teachers, administrators, counselors, family members, and college personnel engage high school educators in understanding the complexities of the lives of working class,

Table 1.1. Youth Participant Demographics

Name	House	Gender	Race/ Ethnicity	Extracurricular Activities in School	College Visit: SU or PU	Future Aspirations
Abigail	G	Female	Black	Yes	PU	Lawyer
Jackie	G	Female	Black	Yes	PU	Lawyer
Melissa	HC	Female	Black	Yes	No	Doctor
Damon	HC	Male	Black	Yes	PU	Stockbroker
Dillon	HC	Male	Black	No	No	Math teacher
Gary	HC-Honors	Male	Black	Yes	PU	Stockbroker
Abraham	HC-Honors	Male	Black	Yes	No	Doctor/Basketball player
Renee	G	Female	Black	Yes	SU	Lawyer/ Accountant
Jason	G	Male	Black	No	No	Doctor
Tracie	G	Female	Black	No	No	Nurse/Doctor
Tamia	HC-Honors	Female	Black	Yes	No	Doctor
Tenisha	G-Honors	Female	Black	Yes	SU	Veterinarian
Dante	G	Male	Black	No	PU	Actor

Table 1.1. Youth Participant Demographics (continued)

Name	House	Gender	Race/ Ethnicity	Extracurricular Activities in School	College Visit: SU or PU	Future Aspirations
Derek	HC	Male	Black	Yes	No	Performing Arts
Richard	G	Male	Black	Yes	SU	Accountant
Perry	G	Male	Black	Yes	No	DJ/Undecided
Andre	HC-Honors	Male	Latino	Yes	PU	Business/Baseball
Jorge	G	Male	Latino	No	No	Accounting
Juan	G	Male	Latino	No	PU	Lawyer
Jesus	HC	Male	Latino	No	No	Undecided
Crystal	G	Female	Latina	No	SU	Psychologist
Marisa	G	Female	Latina	No	PU	Lawyer
Raquel	G	Female	Latina	Yes	SU	Actress
Jessica	HC	Female	Black	No	PU	Physical Therapist/ Choreographer
Yadira	HC	Female	Black/Latina	Yes	No	Psychologist

Note: G = General; HC = Health Careers; SU = State University; PU = Private University.

Black and Latina/o youth, and the everyday teaching and learning practices they encounter in school. In highlighting the voices of youth and their families and school personnel, we provide insight into the necessary shift away from traditional notions of individual counselors as responsible for preparing students for college toward a schoolwide, culturally relevant, college-going culture in which all teachers, counselors, and administrators partner together to assist students in becoming college-ready and attending college. Their perspectives inform what supports or hinders youth's educational experiences.

OVERVIEW OF CONTENTS

The remaining chapters in this book begin with the research findings of the study as related to a particular area of focus with critical "Reading in Action" reflection questions embedded throughout the chapter. These questions ask educators to reflect upon, examine, and analyze their own thoughts, ideas, values, assumptions, and practices about college access within the school or classroom. The research findings are followed by a "Teacher Response" written by Joanne Marciano, a doctoral student who has spent more than 10 years working as a high school teacher in an urban public school serving approximately 500 students in grades 6–12. The

Figure 1.1. Black and Latina/o Youth's Influences for Culturally Relevant College Readiness and Access

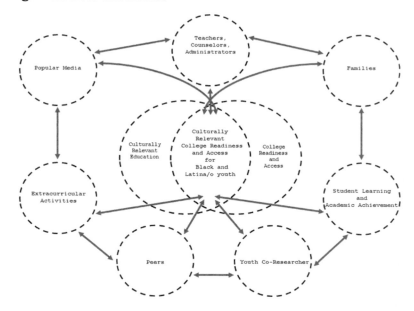

school is similar to Evergreen High School demographically, with Black and Latina/o students comprising 73% and 25% of the study body respectively, and 81% of students eligible for free or reduced lunch (New York State Education Department, 2012). The "Teacher Response" creates a connection between the contents of each chapter while providing insights into a current urban educator's experiences and pedagogical practices working with youth. By further contextualizing how culturally relevant practices can support youth's college readiness and access, the "Teacher Response" serves as a guide for readers to think about how their own experiences and practices in schools may relate to the contents of the book. The chapters end by outlining recommendations and discussion questions for the professional development of individual educators, small groups of educators, and whole school communities, specifically designed to support pre-service and inservice teachers, administrators, and counselors in their efforts to partner together to create, plan, and sustain a college preparation culture in their schools that is culturally relevant. For example, the "Questions and Actions for Individuals" sections describe independent writing and reflection activities for teachers, guidance counselors, support staff, and administrators. The "Recommendations for Small Groups" sections offer discussion questions for small groups of adults including grade-level and content area teams to consider together. The "Recommendations for Large Groups" sections suggest questions entire school communities may consider together as they strive to create a schoolwide culture that supports the college-going aspirations of all students.

CHAPTER 2

It's (Not) Too Early
Negotiating Mixed Messages

You have chosen a school with exceptionally high standards, and we will hold each student to the highest expectations. Choose the most rigorous, demanding and challenging program you can handle. Your future success depends on the hard work you do to achieve your objectives.

—Excerpted from Evergreen High School Student/Parent
Handbook and Course Catalog

Why push going to college if the parents are saying, well you're not going to college, you're going to go to work. Or we'll figure that out in a couple of years. We don't have the money now to talk about this. They're not planning like that.

—Ms. Carson, White, science teacher

I cannot stress it enough to you how important an education is in a person's life. We speak of college quite often at home so you may get used to the idea of attending.

—Jorge's mother, Latina

Well, I've been the college advisor since February 1st . . . one of the reasons is that I was already effectively doing some . . . guidance [as an English teacher] in terms of helping students with college essays. And that was done voluntarily because I wanted to. After school, on my time. And I love doing it because it's something I'm happy to contribute my skills [to] . . . this is a learning experience and I love interacting with the kids. Let me give it a try.

—Ms. Mickelson, White, college advisor

The [teachers] just tell me I know you can do better, so pay attention more. So, that's what I'm going to do now, because I really didn't do so well on the first marking period. I've just got to step it up.

—Darian, Black, male student

The expectations teachers, counselors, administrators, family members, and college admissions officials have of students are integral to the earliest decisions youth make about college and the options they see for themselves. As the quotes above begin to demonstrate, however, youth are often left to negotiate mixed and contradictory messages about whether they are perceived as college bound. At Evergreen High School, for example, the school's mission statement vaguely states it will prepare students for the 21st century, leaving one to imagine what exactly that means. One teacher describes a school culture where overburdened guidance counselors are destined to fail, and another engages a deficit-oriented view of youth's families as uncaring about their education. At the same time, the mother of a youth participant describes how she supports her son in preparing to attend college. We choose to focus on tensions arising between the expectations expressed to youth and the uneven implementation of policies and resources in order to point toward the ways teachers, counselors, and administrators can engage culturally relevant practices to best facilitate college access for Black and Latina/o youth. Just as teachers who engage culturally relevant pedagogies in their classrooms maintain and express high expectations for their students' achievement (Ladson-Billings, 2002), we argue that guidance counselors, administrators, and college admissions officials also can engage in culturally relevant pedagogy as they work with youth and their families in support of students' engagement in college-going practices.

Throughout the chapter, we focus on the "college talk" (Jarsky, McDonough, & Nunez, 2002) that takes place between students and the adults they encounter at school or while on college campus tours. Defined as "ongoing communications with students so that they understand what is required and expected of them if they want to stay on a college path" (p. 362), the "college talk" many youth engage in with adults offers contradictory messages and perceptions. Inconsistent messages about whether or not youth are perceived as capable of attending college pose challenges to increasing college access for Black and Latina/o youth, many of whom rely on their teachers, guidance counselors, and administrators for information about preparing for and applying to college (Smith, 2001). Youth who engage with adults sending contradictory messages to their expectations of attending college may incorrectly assume a postsecondary education is beyond their reach.

A particularly insightful example of a contradictory message is provided by considering how Evergreen High School teachers responded to the researchers' request that they nominate college-bound students as potential participants for the study upon which this text is based. Although official school documents from Evergreen High School, including its mission statement, position the school as one that prepares all of its students for academic success, teachers, counselors, and school personnel said only students enrolled in particular houses, or honors tracks, within the school could be recognized as potential participants. Such sentiments were not lost upon students. Several youth nominated to participate in the study doubted that adults within their school would identify them as college bound. Perry, a Black male participant, for example, said that even though he aspired to attend college, none of his teachers thought that he was capable of doing so. Perry reasoned that it must have been his football coach who recommended him to participate in the study. Perry's assumption points to the ways in which students look beyond their guidance counselors to develop perceptions about their college-going futures. Teachers, coaches, administrators, and additional school personnel together inform students' considerations of college preparation and access. This is particularly important to note when we consider the contexts in which youth are perceived as college bound. Although the Evergreen High School mission statement, for example, alludes to the preparation of all students for college, Perry demonstrates how he negotiates the mixed messages sent about whether or not he is capable of doing so. Of particular concern is that Perry does not think that his teachers, the very people tasked with preparing him for the academic rigor of college, believe he can or will attend. When youth believe their teachers do not perceive them as college bound, as Perry states, doubts may emerge about their college aspirations.

Resolving the tension between schoolwide policies focusing on preparing youth for college and interactions between staff and youth that suggest otherwise becomes imperative in creating an inclusive, culturally relevant, college-going high school culture. If school personnel are able to come together in support of the development of youth's college-going identities, possibilities emerge for increasing college readiness and college access. Youth's negotiations of these mixed and contradictory messages form the basis of this chapter, as we look at the role that (1) formal school policy, (2) teachers and counselors, (3) families, and (4) college admissions personnel play in youth's engagement (or not) in college-going practices.

EXPECTATIONS WITHIN FORMAL
SCHOOL POLICY STATEMENTS

Evergreen High School's mission statement provides a glimpse into how a formal policy statement made by the school articulates its expectations that students attend college. The mission statement, as printed in a school-created document describing Evergreen High School, reads:

> We, the parents, students, staff, alumni, and other supporters of excellence at Evergreen High School believe that high expectations and high standards yield high achievement in both the academic and personal elements of life. All members of the Evergreen community join in the covenant of scholarship and honor that will ensure that all students master the world class standards of knowledge and personal integrity that will be needed in the twenty-first century. In order to achieve these goals, Evergreen High School is undergoing a unique and major restructuring initiative in which our students will enjoy the intimacy of a Small Learning Community and diversity of academic and extra curricular activities that only a large comprehensive high school can offer.
> —Evergreen High School mission statement

While the document goes on to include the comments of an administrator who states that the school was named "an outstanding high school in America," that Evergreen is the school of choice in New York City, and that "over 95% of our graduates were accepted to college," there is no mention of college going in the mission statement itself. Further, as previously stated, students enrolled in some of the small learning communities, or houses, at Evergreen High School were not perceived by all school personnel as college bound—a message youth participants said they received. As a result, youth were often left to negotiate vague messages that their enrollment at Evergreen would lead them to meet the needs of the 21st century, while engaging in "college talk" with teachers who may not have expressed expectations that students, especially those in 9th and 10th grades or those tracked into particular learning communities, were college bound. Additionally, school personnel miss an opportunity, in the mission statement, to recognize and build upon the cultures of the predominantly Black and Latina/o students attending the school. The only mention of diversity refers to the variety of academic and extracurricular activities available at the school due to its size, rather than the rich cultural backgrounds upon which students imagine and enact their futures. We do not mean to suggest that youth's cultural backgrounds must be explicitly named in a school's mission statement in order for school policy to be considered culturally relevant. However, as a public statement of what the school intends for its students to accomplish, the mission statement provides an opportunity to recognize and build upon the varied experiences of youth in preparing them to attend college.

📖 Reading in Action 📖

1.   Refer to the quotes at the beginning of the chapter and reflect on how the expectations represented in these quotes compare with your own experiences.
2.   How do the policies and practices you enact in your role as administrator, teacher, or counselor explicitly reflect high expectations of Black and Latina/o youth as college bound?
3.   How do school documents, such as the mission statement of your school or lesson plans, reflect expectations of youth's engagement in college-going practices?

EXPECTATIONS OF TEACHERS AND GUIDANCE COUNSELORS AT EVERGREEN HIGH SCHOOL

Among the tips for success at Evergreen High School mentioned in the Student/Parent Handbook and Course Catalog was the suggestion that students needed "to get off to a good start from day one! Don't think freshman year doesn't count. It does!" (p. 38). The handbook also provided a checklist that urged 9th-graders to become familiar with college requirements for a range of postsecondary options and to create a 4-year high school curriculum plan. However, written policies within the handbook were at odds with many youth, who expressed the thought that "college talk" often was engaged in with teachers and guidance counselors upon reaching 11th and 12th grades. This tension between policy and practice becomes problematic for 9th-graders who understood the importance of engaging in college-going practices, including "college talk," well before their junior year in high school. The following conversation between Michelle and two youth participants during a small-group discussion serves as an example:

> *Michelle*: Some people say freshman year is too early to start talking about college, right?
>
> *First student*: It's not . . . because the year goes by quick, and then by the time you turn around, it's time for college and you don't know jack.

Second student: Because there's a lot of people that, they don't think about college until senior year. And then when we get out of high school, they don't know what colleges are good, they don't think about college.

These youth's understandings of the need for early awareness and preparation for college going highlight the role of students' own educational expectations and need for planning for college, especially as many of them were negotiating the process as first-generation college goers. Their understandings are supported by research literature demonstrating the importance of beginning college preparation much earlier than 11th grade. Researchers have found that students who attend college often begin to engage in a college preparatory curriculum in 8th grade (Somers, Cofer, & VanderPutten, 2002). For students who attend high schools that do not engage a college preparatory curriculum for all students, there is a possibility that youth will enroll in a curriculum that merely prepares them to meet less rigorous, minimum requirements for graduation rather than engage in rigorous coursework that also prepares them to meet college entrance requirements. If a student in such a school decided in 11th or 12th grade to pursue a college education, there is a likelihood that he or she would not have completed the courses typically deemed necessary in order to pursue higher education.

In schools with high expectations that all students will attend college, school policies and enacted practices can assist students in preparing for college, even if the students themselves may not be aware of it. For example, McDonough's (1997) research focuses on the similarities and differences in college-going practices between students in working class and those in upper class communities. She describes the experiences of one student who did not actively consider attending college until she was in 11th grade. However, the student benefited from her high school's alignment of its curriculum with the entrance requirements of most 4-year colleges. Had the student attended a high school in which students were not perceived as capable of attending college, she might not have engaged in a rigorous curriculum in support of her aspirations to continue her education. Even as researchers, and youth themselves, articulate the importance of preparing for college before 11th grade, many school personnel, including those at Evergreen High School, miss out on opportunities to engage in "college talk" with youth beginning in 9th grade. Such talk is particularly important for Black and Latina/o youth from working class communities, especially those who aspire to be the first in their families to attend college and who typically have less access to information about college (Somers, Cofer, & VanderPutten, 2002). While today's Common Core Standards (2011) begin to lay the groundwork for supporting youth in gaining college access from a curricular standpoint across high school grade levels, adults' expectations for students continue to play a role in supporting youth's engagement in college-going activities in 9th and 10th grades. A teacher, Ms. Wellingford, noted:

> When they come into the school they are told this is what is expected of them . . . students don't rise to low expectations, they rise to high expectations and I think that is an important part of it. (Ms. Wellingford, White, English teacher and director of The Learning Center)

As important a role as teacher expectations may play in supporting youth's access to college, 9th- and 10th-grade students at Evergreen High School had limited opportunities to engage in college-going practices at school. The norms and expectations regarding which Evergreen High School students needed information about college were focused on the 11th- and 12th-graders, and school policies and program offerings were unevenly distributed throughout the school. For example, flyers posted throughout the school, daily schoolwide announcements, and messages from the school's Parent Teacher Association encouraged 11th-grade students to attend Evergreen High School's college fair. Although students in 9th and 10th grades also would likely have benefited from attending the college fair, an announcement made at a PTA meeting clearly stated that 9th- and 10th-grade students were not welcome to attend, in order to ensure that there would be enough room in the gym, where the fair was to be held, for the 11th-graders.

The exclusion of 9th- and 10th-grade students from the college fair at Evergreen High School was not the only example of "college talk" being directed primarily at the 11th- and 12th-grade students attending the school. As one teacher stated:

> The counselors are always giving me notices [about applications] . . . I have to put in, though, that they only do that for seniors. They don't focus on any kind of career orientation for the freshmen. For the freshmen it's mostly adjusting to high school life. (Ms. Carson, White, science teacher)

It is not surprising that teachers expect that guidance counselors are primarily responsible for informing students about college-going processes, as traditional assumptions position guidance counselors in that role. Another teacher considers the high student to counselor ratio at the school as cause for limiting access to information about college for students in 9th and 10th grades.

> Imagine being a guidance counselor and having to know personally a hundred, two hundred, three hundred kids, personally, down to what each student is doing and each student is feeling. I mean, how could

they possibly keep on top of that? There's not enough. There's not enough people. The kids don't get enough individual attention . . . I think, again, our counselors are obviously underpaid and overworked. (Ms. Smith, White, music teacher)

From these two teachers' perspectives, it is up to the school's guidance counselors to develop relationships with students and engage school policies and practices that promote college access. However, the role of the guidance counselor varies across high schools in the United States (McDonough, 2005; Perna, Rowan-Kenyon, Thomas, Anderson, & Li, 2008), and the large student to counselor ratio, which can reach as high as 730 to 1 in large urban cities (Tierney, Corwin, & Colyar, 2005), does not permit school faculty to be the only staff responsible for influencing youth's college-going processes in the high school. Understanding these realities of counselors in urban contexts speaks to the ways in which teachers, counselors, and administrators (re)conceptualize their roles in youth's college-going processes as early as 9th grade. By recognizing the importance of supporting youth in college-going practices beginning in 9th grade, school personnel engage the sociopolitical consciousness of culturally relevant pedagogy (Ladson-Billings, 2002). Rather than hope that students arrive in 11th and 12th grades with the skills and knowledge needed to successfully apply for and enroll in college, school personnel should play an active role in developing and supporting youth's college aspirations throughout their high school years, challenging traditional notions that school counselors alone are singularly charged with preparing all students to enroll in college. For example, just as culturally relevant pedagogical practices may focus on the development of literacy practices among Black students with sociopolitical consideration of the struggle for literacy experienced by their ancestors (Ladson-Billings, 1994a), school personnel must understand the historical barriers to college access, including a lack of information about college-going processes for Black and Latina/o youth, and work to overcome them.

EXPECTATIONS OF AND ABOUT FAMILIES

Of the 27 family members interviewed as part of the research study, 26 expressed the expectation that their child could attend college, disrupting normative assumptions that working class Black and Latina/o families do not support education or encourage their children to attend college. As 9th-graders, in particular, youth recalled words from family members such as, "you know you are going to college," and "I don't care where you go to college, you are going away." When youth asked their family members, "How do you support me going to college?" the responses they received revealed

> ### 📖 Reading in Action 📖
>
> 1.   Can you describe an experience in which you as a teacher, counselor, or administrator engaged in "college talk" to promote college readiness and college access with Black and Latina/o youth?
> 2.   Do you think it is too early for 9th-grade students to prepare for high school? Why or why not?
> 3.   What differences emerge between school documents reflecting college information and access and the "college talk" that takes place between you and your colleagues and students?

the ways in which families extend academic considerations to include connections between the mind, body, and spirit (Siddle Walker & Tompkins, 2004). For example, one mother stated:

> I support you emotionally, physically, financially in every way that a parent possibly can. I encourage you to go [to college] and motivate you into getting your goals. (Jackie's mother, Black)

Similarly, another student's mother noted:

> While I attended college, I would always involve you with my own classwork. You know that and study. We would sit in the living room and after I would study you would ask me questions to see if I had learned anything. Little did you know that I was killing two birds with one stone. You, too, also learned about SBAs—small business administration—as well as tariffs. . . . You did quite well I might add. (Jorge's mother, Latina)

These mothers echo existing research that highlights the important role family members play in developing and nurturing their children's college-going aspirations and expectations (Auerbach, 2004; Knight, Norton, Bentley, & Dixon, 2004; McDonough, 2005; Tierney, Corwin, & Colyar, 2005). For many of the youth participants, their families supported them in choosing to attend Evergreen High School because they thought doing so would prepare the students to attend college. Youth and their families cited the school's reputation for sending students to college, its numerous sports teams, and extensive extracurricular activities as evidence that Evergreen would provide an excellent education and the opportunity to attend college.

For example, Juan's mother stated:

> Evergreen offers many opportunities to succeed through non-for-profit organizations, which will allow you to have a broader selection in industries. For example, ROTC, accounting classes, computer classes, as well as some type of medical studies. There are so many much more different programs as well as classes that Evergreen has to offer I just can't mention them all. (Juan's mother, Puerto Rican)

All of the houses or small learning communities within Evergreen are organized around themes, with a core academic curriculum as well as specialized courses related to the school's capacity to provide opportunities for students to explore varied career options. In describing opportunities at Evergreen that will "allow you to have a broader selection in industries," Juan's mother makes a connection between her son's attendance at the school and his future success. She is clearly aware of some of the programs available at Evergreen to support her son and demonstrates an explicit interest in her son's education. Similarly, Jackie's aunt notes, "Evergreen has lots of programs that influence you to go to college." Both women articulate their expectations that youth will attend college and that their attendance at Evergreen High School will support them in doing so. Therefore, they believe the core academic and career exploration courses provide opportunities for youth's college readiness for a wide variety of careers and access to a range of postsecondary institutions. Even in the current economic downturn, those with bachelor's degrees earned twice as much as those without a high school degree (U.S. Department of Education, 2012).

Moreover, the principal of Evergreen High School also notes in the Student/Parent Handbook that students engaged in extracurricular activities tend to be more successful in high school. Through their participation in extracurricular activities within the school, for instance, youth may develop relationships with school personnel who will then be able to write the in-depth recommendation letters required as part of the college application process. Students who participate in extracurricular activities at Evergreen High School also are able to demonstrate their commitment to engaging as members of their school community, a characteristic of many successful college applicants (Tierney, Corwin, & Colyar, 2005).

Yet the messages of high expectations and college going that youth received from their families were often in conflict with the messages they received from school personnel, many of whom revealed their assumptions that parents were not active influences in the lives of students. Such a perceived lack of influence on the part of parents left some teachers to assume 9th grade was too early to engage in "college talk" with youth. For example, one teacher attributed teachers' failure to talk with 9th-grade students about college-going practices to a lack of parental influence.

> *Michelle*: I have the impression that a lot of people think 9th grade is too early [to talk about college going]. And yet, in a lot of other settings people would say 9th grade is too late.
>
> *Ms. Carson*: True.
>
> *Michelle*: It's very interesting which settings you're in when people say 9th grade is too early.
>
> *Ms. Carson*: Here they would say 9th grade is too early.
>
> *Michelle*: Right.
>
> *Ms. Carson*: Only because a lot of 9th-graders are not at the level. I'd say the majority. They're not at the level to, let's say, pass a Regents test. So they try to focus on writing skills, reading skills, and things like that. In another setting, it may be appropriate because the parents are urging it. So I think for the most part it's how the parents are stressing it at home. So, if the parents are not stressing it at home, we've got to get the parents involved in it. And so the parents—the PTA meetings—right now what we're doing, the principal is bringing in the assistant principals to the parents association to explain to the parents what the students need to do to graduate. Because a lot of them don't know. They really don't. And most of them don't come to those meetings. So you can see where we're at.
>
> *Michelle*: Right.
>
> *Ms. Carson*: Why push going to college if the parents are saying, well you're not going to college, you're going to go to work? Or we'll figure that out in a couple of years. We don't have the money now to talk about this. They're not planning like that.

Ms. Carson's assumption that the working class families of Evergreen High School's Black and Latina/o student body are not engaging in "college talk" with their children echoes the sentiments of a number of teachers in the study who expressed similar views. Some also stated their belief that attending a local or state college was not in the best interests of the students, despite cultural norms of Latina/o and Black families that may lead them to see such institutions as particularly attractive (Gonzalez, Stoner, & Jovel, 2003). Yet, in family interviews, parents of 9th-graders expressed how they thought Evergreen would provide support in addition to the ways they supported their children. For example, Abigail's mother told her daughter, "I think the school supports you by tell[ing] you what is required from you to get into the college you want to go to." Damon's mother said, "I support you by keeping on encouraging you so that you can succeed in college, financial support, [and] physical support." The differences between the messages youth received about college going from family members and from many of their teachers left youth to negotiate mixed messages about how families thought the school was supporting their child, teachers' low expectations of them as college bound, and the high expectations that their families had for them to go to college.

Engaging in culturally relevant practices that forefront the strengths of youth and their families may lead to more consistent messages of college going for youth, demonstrating the expectation that 9th grade is not too early to engage in "college talk." By communicating more effectively with youth and their families about college-going practices, educators can better understand the divergent views and mixed messages students are receiving about their identities as college-bound youth. Understanding these mixed messages can enable educators to provide clear and high expectations and to enact culturally relevant practices that, in concert with students' families, support Black and Latina/o youth's learning opportunities, their college aspirations, and eventually their access to a range of postsecondary institutions.

📖 Reading in Action 📖

1. In what ways do the expectations of and about families described in this chapter reflect (or not) your own experiences in school?
2. Are the teachers', guidance counselors', and administrators' expectations for youth's college readiness and college access, as described in this chapter and in your own experiences, the same for all families? Why or why not?
3. How do you engage culturally relevant policies and practices to find out about families' college-going expectations for youth? How can families' expectations that youth attend college be supported?

EXPECTATIONS OF COLLEGE CAMPUS PERSONNEL

Traditional notions of the college application process often consider 11th grade as the time when students should tour college campuses with their families and meet admissions officials before choosing which colleges to apply to during the fall of their senior year. This linear process, in which 12th-grade students send out college applications in the fall and receive acceptance letters in the spring before high school graduation is often reflective of the experiences of middle and upper class students, particularly those whose parents attended college (McDonough, 2005; Sacks, 2007; Tierney, 2009). For example, McDonough (1997) describes affluent students whose parents fly them across the country to visit the campuses of colleges they may be interested in seeking admission to. Yet working class Black and Latina/o students often experience the college application process in a much more cyclical fashion, sometimes making decisions about whether or not to apply to college as late as the spring of their senior year in high school (Tierney, 2009). For these students, an introduction to college-going practices that begins well before their entrance into 11th and 12th grades may create opportunities to develop college-going identities and to seek out opportunities to visit college campuses, even if their families are not familiar with such practices (Somers, Cofer, & VanderPutten, 2002).

Providing opportunities for Black and Latina/o youth to tour college campuses beginning in 9th grade offers them information about the expectations college admissions officials have of students, the importance of academic and extracurricular achievements in high school, and how the college fits their cultural and social needs and desires for their lives on campus. Moreover, teachers who are aware of the value of campus visits for 9th-graders can set high expectations and fuel youth's curiosity about what it is like to attend college. With this understanding, teachers can better support not only youth's access to campus visits but a consciousness of the expectations various colleges have for admission, differences between high school and college, and factors leading to retention and graduation of Black and Latina/o students in college. The college visit can become a culturally relevant structure that further supports youth's critical awareness of college-going processes as they take notes or digitally document their visit. Specifically, teachers, counselors, administrators, and youth can draft together some common questions that are relevant to their lives to ask during college visits. Youth can then be better prepared to participate effectively in a range of conversations with college personnel and college students, meeting learning standards for listening and speaking as they do so (Common Core Standards, 2011). School staff also can ensure that students have already been prepared at their high school for understanding the admissions criteria for various colleges. In this way, the college visit is not the first time students hear such information. Rather, the college visit serves as further reinforcement of messages for high academic expectations, college readiness, and student inquiry on such topics as scholarships and the social life and campus culture that are important and relevant to their lives. A systemic structuring of such information, whether through the counselor's office, advisory period, and/or "college talk" among staff and students, can facilitate these opportunities. After the college visit, students can utilize their notes and pictures taken during the tours to write reflective analytic journals or utilize digital media to share with peers and family members what they experienced and felt about the visit. They also may outline some pros and cons of the college/university around academics, student life and social activities, housing/food, and financial aid, noting similarities and differences between their experiences and what is promoted on the college's website. Through these learning opportunities, students can demonstrate from firsthand experiences what they know about college expectations, readiness, access, and whether the school is a fit for their lives (Common Core Standards, 2011). Peers also can positively encourage one another through informal sharing of their experiences and through formal structures such as a lunch time panel within the school. By connecting the college visit to the curricula of schools, schools can become more culturally relevant in supporting youth's college readiness.

For Evergreen High School students, the norms and expectations regarding who needs to visit colleges and receive college information were focused on the 11th- and 12th-graders. Unfortunately, the message of 9th grade being "too early" once again was sent to students, this time reflected by norms of college policies. Youth participants in the research study, for example, were provided with several opportunities to visit the campuses of local colleges when they were in 9th and 10th grades. The visits were arranged at the request of students, who knew that they did not have the college information that they needed and specifically used their agency to ask whether members of the research team conducting the study would take them to tour local college campuses. Nineteen of the twenty-five youth in the study received permission from their families to attend one of two campus visits jointly sponsored by Evergreen High School and Teachers College, Columbia University. Evergreen High School counselors also attended these visits to obtain college-going information.

During these visits, students continued to negotiate mixed and vague messages of "it's (not) too early," as well as who is "right" for the campus, as reflected in the cultural and political norms of the college admissions "talk," the financial aid "talk," and the college guided tour. These norms undergirded the beliefs and values the institutions wanted to convey about which students are admitted, how they are admitted, and the ways in which they are expected to fulfill the role of a college student on a particular campus (Magolda, 2000). Similar to high school personnel, college personnel also demonstrated high expectations for 11th- and 12th-graders as prospective students, while expressing almost nonexistent expectations for 9th-graders. For example, during one college campus visit, a White male admissions and financial aid officer started his session by asking how many of the Black and Latina/o students were 11th- and 12th-graders. After realizing that students were 9th-graders, he appeared to change his presentation and made several comments about it being "early," before stating, "as you approach your junior and senior year, call us." While college admissions officials typically may focus their attention on prospective students in 11th and 12th grades, younger students most certainly benefit as well from information about what would make them a competitive applicant at a particular college. If "in-depth" and specific information about academic requirements or the importance of participating in extracurricular activities beginning in 9th grade is withheld, some students unknowingly may fail to meet eligibility requirements for college admission.

During another campus visit, an Asian female university admissions officer's talk centered on the higher education application process, the college's selection process, and the outstanding features of the university. Students who attended the tour were told that they would be expected to articulate in their college essay what they could "contribute" and how they would "fit" into the university community. The admissions officer mentioned that the essay was the place for students to have a "direct voice," which "really lets us get a sense of who you are." She went on to emphasize that the essay was the most stressful part of the application process. "If you can tell us everything in a page or two, you're probably a boring person." Throughout the session, she continued to say that the university was "looking for the right kind of student, students who have a predisposition for being active." Although the admissions officer advised one student, who did not participate in extracurricular activities because she needed to work, to write about the experiences gained from her job in a donut shop, we wondered how students interpreted the meanings of "active," "contribute," and "fitting in" at any postsecondary institution. For example, what messages about college going did a Black female and her friend receive when they noticed the absence of Blacks and Latina/os on the campus? The students counted the number of Black people they saw during the campus visit, joking with one another about trying to count people more than once. Later, after finding 20 Black college students, they began to count the Latina/o students they saw. What role did the lack of visibility of Black and/or Latina/o students on campus play in the continued development of the Evergreen students' perceptions of themselves as college-going youth?

The college admissions "talk" students encountered during the campus tours they attended also lacked a focus on specific high school curricular requirements, and an understanding of the constraints that students attending an urban school might face, such as a lack of access to Advanced Placement. The curricular emphasis was placed on taking the most rigorous courses that Evergreen High School had to offer, regardless of students' access to such classes, and the importance of getting recommendation letters from counselors as well as math and English teachers so that college admissions officials could "see students' performance in a quantitative and qualitative setting." Yet, counselors shared the difficulty of writing letters given conditions within the school and colleges' expectations of them. Mrs. Estevez expressed how "colleges want these letters of recommendation from the guidance counselors. You know in New York City we don't know the kids that way. We have guidance counselors in New York City that have a caseload of 500 students. And you're asking that guidance counselor to write a letter for Johnny that she doesn't know."

Youth also were negotiating daily the expectations of college admissions officers along with their own school policies, relationships with teachers and school personnel, and family dynamics as related to college going. Juan, for example, one of the Latino participants, represents several of the students who attended the college tours mentioned above. He is not in 11th or 12th grade, in any of the school programs or classes that his mother mentions are available to him at Evergreen, or taking the most rigorous courses that his school has to offer. Similar to Juan, many of the youth in the study desire to attend college and believe that they are college bound, but actually may not be engaging in the courses or activities that college admissions officials consider necessary for admission. This is partly because of the students' reliance on their own agency to position themselves as college bound in the absence of educators and/or college admissions officials who provide them with information about college-going processes before 11th and 12th grades. For example, after the college visits, Andre wanted to know how he could find out whether he was taking the most challenging courses his school had to offer. Other students remarked how much they wanted to go to college and asked questions about what they needed to do in high school to meet the admissions requirements of a variety of colleges. Still other students became aware that their grades needed to improve and sought out the services of after-school tutors. Other students heard the admissions official's words that students "contribute" something to the college as a call for participating in extracurricular activities in and out of school contexts. The enthusiasm with which students engaged the admissions official's recommendations leads us to only imagine what decisions students may have made about course selection and participation in extracurricular activities as early as 9th grade had they known doing so could support them in attending college.

IMPLICATIONS AND CONCLUSION

High schools across the nation seeking to create a culturally relevant, college-going high school culture for Black and Latina/o youth need to focus on sending clear messages about expectations for college readiness. These messages can be sent through both written school policies at the

---

📖 Reading in Action 📖

1. How could you create culturally relevant teaching and learning opportunities for 9th- and 10th-grade students to engage with college admissions officials at high school fairs or during college visits? ·
2. What opportunities exist for you to develop relationships with college admissions officials to send youth clear expectations about college readiness and college access?
3. What supportive school structures are needed for you to better understand the inequities in college access for Black and Latina/o youth and to act upon them?

---

national, state, and local level, and enacted practices within the relationships between school personnel and students. For example, in the case of written policies, such as the implementation of the Common Core Standards (2011), schools nationwide are being asked to prepare students for college readiness through varied understandings of the different types of knowledge and skills across the curriculum that are needed for access to college. Schools that do not have written college-readiness policies can begin to look at their mission statements and student/parent handbooks to examine how they might better reflect such a stance.

Yet, what we also learn from the youth is that national, state, and local written policies, brought to bear at the school level and focusing on college readiness, are necessary but not sufficient. It is essential that teachers, counselors, and administrators develop relationships with Black and Latina/o youth that emphasize their beliefs that youth are capable of success and perceived as college bound. Acting on these beliefs in their relationships with students, the teachers, counselors, and administrators engage in "college talk," set high expectations, recognize the support of students' families in the college process, and affirm students' college-going aspirations. A school-wide college-going culture that examines the expectations revealed within the "college talk" of formal school policies and the relationships between and among teachers, administrators, counselors, college personnel, youth, and their families can have a powerful impact on the development and nurturance of youth's aspirations and expectations that they will attend college. Access to such culturally relevant practices and policies within schools can prepare and provide opportunities for Black and Latina/o youth to develop their critical consciousness, effectively negotiate varied mixed messages about their college-bound identities and preparation for college readiness, and challenge educational inequities they encounter.

TEACHER RESPONSE

As the hallways emptied on the last day of school, several 10th-grade students stood at their lockers examining their report cards. When I asked whether they were pleased with their grades, Inez responded first, handing over a report card with a GPA in the mid-80s. I congratulated her and said I hoped to see her in the 11th-grade English class I'd teach the following year. Inez smiled at first, but when I mentioned the course focused on writing techniques useful in college, she shook her head. Her parents couldn't afford to pay for college, she explained. There was no way she could go. Unfortunately, Inez's assumption that college is too expensive to be an option for her future is held by many working class students, particularly those who would be the first in their families to attend college. Such students often lack the cultural capital typically afforded to youth whose parents, family members, and/or neighbors attended college and are able to share their experiences, including strategies for paying for college. As Inez demonstrates, however, a lack of information about financial aid among working class youth may generate low expectations for college going.

The traditional expectations of teachers, counselors, and administrators that 9th and 10th grades are too early to begin engaging students in "college talk," coupled with the high caseloads experienced by many guidance counselors in working class schools who typically are seen as singularly responsible for sharing information about college, often contribute to the lack of information that leaves youth to independently negotiate mixed messages of college expectations, including questions of how to pay for college. For Inez, that meant considering my expectation that she attend college, her own expectation that attending college would place too much of a financial burden on her family, and the expectations of her family members, other teachers, guidance counselors, and school administrators. For even as school personnel often perceive students in 9th and 10th grades as too young to engage in "college talk," the students themselves—and their families—often think otherwise (Bonous-Hammarth & Allen, 2004). The parents of Evergreen High School students, for example, attempt to disrupt traditional deficit-oriented views portraying them as not caring about their children's education. Yet even as parents and families demonstrate high expectations for youth's college-going futures, the silence of school personnel who view 9th- and 10th-grade students as too young to engage in "college talk" has the potential to leave youth thinking a college education is out of reach.

Students at Evergreen High School demonstrate the effectiveness of visiting college campuses as one technique for facilitating "college talk" among school personnel and 9th- and 10th-grade students. As Juan, Andre, and their classmates demonstrate in this chapter, campus tours provide an opportunity for youth to envision themselves as college students and ask questions about what they might do to emerge as competitive applicants. For working class youth, particularly those who hope to be the first in their families to attend college, opportunities to visit college campuses, engage with current college students, and ask questions of admissions officials and professors, may help to sort out many of the mixed messages and expectations students receive about attending college. Unlike for many of their White peers of higher socioeconomic status backgrounds whose families, friends, and neighbors likely attended college, school trips to visit college campuses often provide Black and Latina/o working class urban youth with their first opportunities to see college for themselves and to challenge normative assumptions of college going about which they have received conflicting messages throughout their lives. While school personnel who work with 9th- and 10th-grade students may need to develop the sociopolitical consciousness necessary to challenge the tendencies of college officials to promote campus visits for only 11th- and 12th-grade students, such visits have the potential to provide valuable information to students that may change the way 9th- and 10th-grade students engage in schooling. If, as Andre and his classmates indicate, a visit to a college campus can encourage students to "contribute" to their school community, improve their grades, or enroll in challenging courses, consider what happens when youth are not aware of how such practices impact their access to college. Would Inez have engaged differently in school if she'd realized college was within her reach? Might she have participated in more rigorous coursework or extracurricular activities if she knew doing so would make her a more competitive applicant? Would information about financial aid have challenged her expectation that she did not have enough money to attend college? Such questions are further complicated for students who enter 9th and 10th grades eager to attend college, yet who leave school before reaching 11th grade when "college talk" typically is initiated by school personnel.

To create a culturally relevant, schoolwide, college-going culture that includes 9th- and 10th-grade students, all those who work with youth must actively engage in "college talk" that centers on consistent messages of positive expectations, affirms college going as a goal toward which to strive, and provides the information and support necessary to make that goal a reality. Yet in many schools, including Evergreen High School, the responsibility of guiding students through the college preparation and application process is placed squarely on the shoulders of the school's guidance counselor(s), many of whom are already burdened with extraordinarily high caseloads. Such traditional views of the guidance counselor as sole purveyor of information about college must be disrupted if students, particularly those in 9th and 10th grades, are to benefit from engaging in "college talk." Because the messages of expectation related to college going we send to working class youth are necessarily informed by our own schooling experiences, I suggest we first must consider our own schooling experiences and expectations related to attending college, in order to work toward the development of a schoolwide culture that supports college going. We also must consider the perspectives and experiences of our colleagues. Before groups of adults may effectively engage in conversations about how to best support the college-going practices of youth, they first must consider the varying perspectives from which they view college going. While there are a number of ways to engage in such consideration, the questions below, and those that appear at the ends of Chapters 3–6, are starting points for reflection, discussion, and action.

Questions and Actions for Individuals

1.   Describe your own academic experience in high school. Were you considered a "good" student? Why or why not? Who or what sent you messages of expectation about your academic performance? What were those expectations? Did you agree or disagree with them? Why? What messages of academic expectation did your peers receive? Why?

2.   What was the reputation of the high school you attended? Where was it located? How many students attended? Why did they attend? What were the cultural and economic backgrounds of the students in the school? How were cultural and economic similarities and differences reflected in the curriculum and/or expectations of school personnel?

3.   When did you decide that you would attend college? How did you come to that decision? Who and/or what supported that decision? Who and/or what presented challenges to that decision? What messages of expectation did you receive about being college bound from your school, family, friends, and neighbors? Who in your school did not attend college? Why? What messages of expectation might they have received from school personnel?

Questions and Actions for Small Groups
Within School Communities

1.   Consider the messages of academic achievement sent to youth in your school. Which students are considered "good" students? Why? What expectations do you and other adults have for them? What expectations do you have for other students? How are those expectations delivered? Are they articulated through direct instruction, "college talk," messages posted throughout the school,

or additional means? How are those expectations perceived by youth?

2.   How do you perceive your role in preparing youth to attend college? Why? Discuss your most recent engagement in "college talk" with students and adults in your school. Who was involved in the conversations? How were the conversations initiated? Were the conversations informed by students' perceptions of college going? What expectations were relayed in the "college talk"? Are such expectations consistent with those sent by other school personnel, students, their families, and their peers?

3.   Compare the Evergreen High School mission statement in this chapter with the following mission statement taken from the Bronx High School of Science:

> The Bronx High School of Science attracts an intellectually gifted blend of culturally, ethnically and economically diverse students. Scienceites, as the school's students are known, are supported by an actively involved Parents' Association, Alumni Association and a core of master teachers who excel at their craft. Our students are proud of their school's alumni who include: seven Nobel Prize winners, the first African-American neurosurgeon, countless authors, lawyers, physicians, educators, artists, entertainers and leaders in business and government. . . . We are the ideal school for all who seek a rigorous college preparatory program and wish to learn in an environment committed to educational excellence. (http://www.bxscience. edu/mission.jsp)

4.   What are the similarities and differences between the two statements and their focus on college readiness and access for all students?

Questions and Actions for Whole-School Communities

1.   Take an inventory of the existing school structures, policies, and practices that support a college-going culture, such as youth's access to computers to search for college admissions information, culturally relevant curriculum that presents Black and Latina/o youth as college bound, and access to a college counseling center. Look, for example, at your school's mission statement. What is it? How/why was it developed? Do the school mission and other policies, such as who gets access to the most academically rigorous courses, support a schoolwide culture of consistent college-going expectations for all students? Why or why not? Are the actual expectations students

encounter consistent with the expectations set forth in the school's mission statement and other policies? Why or why not?

2.   When and how do students currently receive information about college? Is information available to students at all grade levels? Are school personnel aware of the expectations students receive from their families and communities related to college going? What opportunities exist to further inform students and their families about college?

3.   How might the school community begin to develop or strengthen the goal that clear communication of high expectations and a college-going culture is implemented for all students? Who is responsible for developing and maintaining consistent messages of college expectation? For example, what role will the teachers, counselors, and administrators play in sending these clear messages to students and their families? How might students be encouraged to challenge the mixed messages of expectation they encounter about preparing for and attending college?

CHAPTER 3

Promoting College Readiness Through Teachers' and Counselors' Culturally Relevant Pedagogies

I can show you some of the portraiture things that are there outside. The Busta Rhymes face, one in a bandana with a Puerto Rican flag. He's not Puerto Rican! But it's cool, I mean. It expresses itself all the time. Whenever I say, you have freedom to do whatever you like. Whatever image you want. *Bam.* The flag. The flag. It's the first thing that comes up. It [their culture] expresses itself all the time. And that's from Kindergarten all the way up, to college for Christ's sake. It's normal, you identify, you know you're expressing who you are. It happens all the time.

—Mr. Cortez, Puerto Rican, art teacher

I think the idea of wanting something better for themselves in the future than what they have right now. I think there's much more of an impetus for the kids in our school than there was for, let's say, me, in my school. I was in a middle to upper middle class suburb in northern New York. And it was like a given. So you go to college, you know. No big deal. But I think they have much more of an incentive. They're much more hungry. . . . Because they want something they don't have.

—Ms. Martin, White, counselor

The English teacher wants everybody to go to college. He likes to teach [my class] because we have a lot of potential.

—Jessica, Latina, student

At Evergreen, they are having people from different colleges come into the school and talk to us about college and give us different [views] and just hand out information. They gave us the opportunity to get to know a college or how to prepare for college.

—Riley, Black, male student

Jessica, Riley, Mr. Cortez, and Ms. Martin, in the quotations above, offer insight into their beliefs and practices about staff and youth's racialized and class identities and youth's cultural expressions and aspirations to attend college. Similarly, Geneva Gay (2010), who writes about culturally responsive practices, describes how "culture determines how we think, believe, and behave, and these, in turn, affect how we teach and learn" (p. 9). Therefore, conscious awareness of the connection between culture and education bears further examination. The ways teachers and counselors understand how their own and their students' cultures affect the educational process, especially how they build on working class Black and Latina/o youth's lives and cultural backgrounds and identities to support their college readiness and access, are essential. Research has shown that students who are taught by teachers who use culturally relevant instructional practices and policies, which recognize and center race and ethnicity, are able to achieve academically while maintaining their cultural identities (Gay, 2010; Howard, 2001; Ladson-Billings, 1994a; Lipman, 1996). Specifically, guidance counselors, teachers, and administrators support Black and Latina/o students' college aspirations and readiness while building upon their cultural identities and assets such as bilingualism, social or religious values, and community ethics (Tierney, Corwin, & Colyar, 2005). Conversely, when educators work through a culturally neutral or colorblind framework that does not "see" color (Gay, 2010; Thompson, 1998), educators may not recognize the cultural contextual factors, specifically race, that influence their relationships with Black and Latina/o students, which in turn often leads to a decrease in student achievement (Valenzuela, 1999). Thus, despite the good intentions of some educators to not see "race," research has shown the positive connection between academic success and affirming students' ethnic and racial identities (Dei, Mazzuca, & McIssac, 1997; Gay, 2010; Jun & Colyar, 2002; Ladson-Billings, 1994a).

Given the impact of teachers' and counselors' beliefs and practices about culture and education, and therefore the learning opportunities and outcomes of Black and Latina/o urban youth, this chapter examines how teachers' and counselors' instructional and curricular practices support and/or hinder youth's college readiness and access. We illustrate how their culturally relevant practices explicitly acknowledge and build upon youth's race and ethnicity to facilitate students' learning by acknowledging, talking about, and supporting their academic achievement, cultural identities, and sociopolitical consciousness. We provide explicit examples of how teachers' and guidance counselors' knowledge of and practices with Black and Latina/o students serve as resources for schoolwide change and college access. Additionally, we highlight guidance counselors' contradictory practices, which at times take into account students' culture and at other times do not see it as relevant to their practice.

TEACHERS: CURRICULUM, CULTURAL IDENTITIES, AND CRITICAL CONSCIOUSNESS

Most teachers at Evergreen High School described a combination of sometimes contradictory culturally relevant and culturally colorblind beliefs and practices that occurred in their classrooms. For instance, while teachers often expressed in interviews their beliefs that their teaching philosophies and practices were culturally relevant, only a few educators' beliefs and practices actually reflected students' cultural backgrounds. Some of the teachers who were able to incorporate culturally relevant pedagogies based on students' ethnic and cultural backgrounds included Ms. Smith and Ms. Abrego, as the examples below will illustrate. While the Common Core Standards (2011) focus on the curriculum for subjects such as English and math, we provide examples from these fine arts teachers to highlight the ways in which teachers across multiple subject areas schoolwide can improve Black and Latina/o youth's educational experiences and support their college readiness and access. Through their daily interactions and practices, the teachers utilized the students' ethnic and racial cultures to (1) support academic achievement in the content area, (2) facilitate development of students' own cultural competencies, and (3) engage students in activities specific to their college-going literacies.

Teacher Focus #1: Ms. Smith (White, Music Teacher and Band Director). Ms. Smith has taught a variety of music courses with freshmen through seniors in every class. In band class, which she has taught for 2 years, Ms. Smith supports students' college readiness by engaging in activities that foreground students' ethnic and racial heritage. In so doing, her practices advance students' academic knowledge of the arts, develop their multicultural college-going identities, and support sociopolitical consciousness by providing the time and place for youth to question stereotypes they hold about one another as well as stereotypes that may be held about them.

> As far as affirming their cultural identities . . . and this is strictly from a band standpoint—once they learn to play, the books that I use . . . have folk songs from all over the world. And the teacher's manual will

give you an actual history of the song, and the composer, and they use African folk songs, they use American folk songs, they use Chinese and Korean folk songs, so as far as affirming their cultural identity, they can start to see what their culture is, what part they had in the music that they're playing, but how it sounds different.

Culturally relevant educators understand their subject matter in depth and their learners so that they can successfully teach the subject matter to a particular group of students (Ladson-Billings, 1995). In this instance, students' cultural identities are supported by teachers, as students extend their knowledge about their own musical heritage, their classmates' musical heritage, and how the music has evolved to its current forms. Ms. Smith also views the music classroom as a place to "eliminate racial stereotypes."

We do listening things at the beginning of the year, where I let them bring in what I call classroom-appropriate music, and we do a lot of different listening. We break down the stereotype—where they don't need to look at me as, Ms. Smith, that's that White lady that teaches music, that doesn't know anything about my hip-hop, or my R&B. Right away, we try to eliminate the fact that they can't tell what kind of music you listen to based on what you look like, that if you're Black, you may not listen to hip-hop and R&B. If you're White, you may not listen to country. If you're Spanish, you may not like listening to salsa. You can't connect culturally a way a person looks with the music that they listen to.

Researchers have noted that celebrating ethnic contributions reflects the most basic level of integrating youth's cultures into school, and educators need to support more inclusive culturally relevant practices (Sleeter & Grant, 2009). Ms. Smith's beliefs and practices go much further in supporting the development of students' academic achievement, cultural competence, and critical consciousness, as they draw upon knowledge of students' own culture and also expand their knowledge about the cultures of their peers. Ms. Smith provides students with multiple opportunities to demonstrate their knowledge and expertise, as well as the chance to explore the multidimensional and changing aspects of culture that occur in every ethnic group. She employs in her practices her beliefs about students' cultural backgrounds and identities as strengths to build on their academic skills, which, in turn, supports their college readiness and success in fields related to music. Moreover, Ms. Smith also elaborates on the ways in which she supports students' college-going literacies (Gildersleeve, 2010). Specifically, she discusses how to support students' financial literacies, which are needed in order to apply for financial aid to go to college.

I helped, filled out countless FAFSAs this last year and the year before
. . . they can't get anything without the FAFSA. No money, no loan, no
scholarship, you can't even get academic-based scholarships without
the FAFSA.

Ms. Smith's decision to support youth in applying for financial aid reflects her understanding of working class students' concerns about paying
for college. In addition to providing academic support for youth, culturally
relevant educators are aware of other factors, or barriers, that need to be addressed for working class youth to attend college. For example, while many
youth do not understand how they will be able to pay for college (Tierney &
Venegas, 2009), culturally relevant educators are aware of important learning experiences that address college readiness and financial aid information
that supports students' access to college.

Teacher Focus #2: Ms. Abrego (Latina, Art Teacher). Ms. Abrego has been
teaching art for 3 years and specifically connects her philosophy of "giving
100 percent" to her concern for her students' development of subject matter expertise and multicultural college-going identities. She discussed how
the freshmen "come in with an attitude" stemming from junior high school
and elementary school, where they received "the wrong impression about
art." She went on to say that because "we give a hundred percent here . . . it
changes their [the students] whole outlook on the arts." Giving 100 percent
means "we don't kick back, we don't sit down and not do anything. We interact with the students, we introduce things that concern other cultures in
the field of arts, we do a lot of hands-on things, keeps them busy."

Specifically, Ms. Abrego's culturally relevant practices are revealed in
her pedagogical practices, which facilitate students' college readiness by
supporting their academic achievement and multicultural college-going
identities. Her practices simultaneously broaden youth's understanding of
their own culture, the cultures of their classmates, and the art activities
needed for them to be college-ready and apply for college. In the following
assignment, Ms. Abrego situates students' diverse cultures as a resource to
bridge home and school cultures and give students access to new knowledge. Moreover, she creates a collaborative learning environment in which
students develop a positive connection with their peers. For example, she
braids together students' cultural backgrounds through an interdisciplinary
project that incorporates art, writing, and poetry.

I do an assignment that involves them bringing in something from their
culture, and speaking about it in class, that way, it enables everybody
to learn about Peruvians, or Dominicans, or Puerto Ricans, or African
Americans, or Jewish people. So we learn from each other, and that's

very important. So, they learn about themselves because they have to do research . . . we do an assignment that needs writing and artwork as well. . . . A calligraphy assignment that involves maybe pictures showing their culture, and then they read the poem, and they tell us what it means to them, and how it brings them closer to their culture.

Similar to Ms. Smith's culturally relevant practices that supported students' college-going identities and strengthened their cultural competence, Ms. Abrego described working one-on-one with a student to create her portfolio for applying to college.

So we're going to work together, and that's exactly what I did, even on weekends. I'd show her how to take her slides, so that when I'm not there, she can do it herself. We made a lot of trips together where we got together, we mounted work—it's not just about putting it on construction paper.

Gildersleeve (2010) contends that students develop college-going literacies when afforded the opportunity to "recognize, critique and re-imagine their own participation in the process" (p. 4). Moreover, through a focus on students' culture that supported the notions of college-going literacies, Ms. Smith's and Ms. Abrego's practices afford these youth such opportunities while promoting their academic achievement, cultural competence, and sociopolitical consciousness as college-bound Black and Latina/o youth.

📖 **Reading in Action** 📖

1. Refer to the quotes at the beginning of the chapter and reflect on the questions these quotes raised for you.
2. In what ways did the fine arts teachers' culturally relevant teaching and learning practices support youth's college readiness and access?
3. How do your understandings of students' cultural backgrounds influence your interactions with Black and Latina/o students in your own school?
4. What are some of the cultural stereotypes about Black and Latina/o youth? In what ways might these stereotypes between and among students and school personnel be challenged?

Researchers have noted the importance of incorporating students' diverse backgrounds into academic and co-curricular activities (Jarksy, McDonough, & Nunez, 2009; Villapando & Solorzano, 2004). Culturally relevant educators such as Ms. Smith and Ms. Abrego center race and ethnicity as a site of learning in their pedagogical practices, opening spaces for youth to achieve academic success, maintain their cultural identities, critique knowledge, and improve their access to college-going opportunities. For urban working class Latina/o and Black college-bound youth, especially first-generation students, teachers' support in the maintenance of a college-going identity takes on added relevance. Because Ms. Smith and Ms. Abrego build upon students' lives and cultures, youth in their classes are able to achieve academic excellence in their subject matter, grow in understanding of and respect for their own cultures and the multiple cultures of their peers, and view the college-going process as critical active learners in understanding college-going literacies (Gildersleeve, 2010). Moreover, in structuring small-group intercultural interactions and building upon students' cultural backgrounds, these teachers provide inclusive perspectives on race and ethnicity that facilitate students' awareness of the knowledge they do have, how they can learn from one another, and their relational competencies and sociocivic skills in an increasingly diverse schooling environment (Gay, 2010). Additionally, the use of culturally relevant practices opens up learning opportunities for teachers and students to engage in critical thinking about, question, and challenge educational and social inequities such as the stereotypes and cultural conflicts stemming from possible discriminatory views they hold in relation to diverse cultural groups. Thus, the teachers' culturally relevant practices engage students in examining the subject matter as a basis for personal and social values.

GUIDANCE COUNSELORS: ADVISING AND FACILITATING STUDENTS' MULTICULTURAL COLLEGE-GOING IDENTITIES

In addition to examining the culturally relevant practices of teachers, it is equally important to understand how guidance counselors do or do not employ a range of culturally relevant practices to facilitate or hinder Black and Latina/o youth's college-going multicultural identities and access to college (Farmer-Hinton, 2006; Oakes, Rogers, Lipton, & Morrell, 2002). Counselors at Evergreen High School employed a range of pedagogical approaches with students. Many of these approaches were general in nature but others were more specific in supporting aspects of youth's identities by focusing on race, ethnicity, and gender. Collectively, in their daily interactions and conversations with youth, the counselors incorporated culturally relevant pedagogical practices and engaged the formation of multicultural college-going identities in three important ways. First, they engaged in "future-oriented" conversations with youth about college information. Second, they shared their own (un)examined norms and expectations for students. Finally, they related their own personal college experiences to connect to Black and Latina/o youth's college-going identities.

Future-Oriented Perspective

A future-oriented perspective and high expectations were demonstrated through counselors' college-going interactions when they would ask students about their career goals, discuss options for the future, collaborate with them in making college choices about location and size, take them on college tours, and write letters of recommendation for them. The following excerpts from interviews with two guidance counselors at Evergreen High School provide examples of how a future-oriented perspective may be implemented in a variety of ways.

Guidance Counselor Focus #1: Mrs. Estevez (Latina). Mrs. Estevez has supported students' college-going aspirations during the 5 years she has spent as a guidance counselor at Evergreen High School. She employs a future-oriented perspective to evaluate students' college-going aspirations. She begins by asking very personal questions of the students and connecting their responses to their home lives, thereby bridging students' home and school cultures.

> I ask them questions like "okay, well, tell me what you want to study, what are you interested in doing?" We talk about geography. Where do you want to go to school? Do you think that you can afford to go to school? Let's look at the possibilities. Have you spoken to your parents? Who do you live with? I try to make it as realistic as possible for the students about their choices. My students make an application to one of the schools here in New York City through the CUNY system. They also make an application to one of the State University of New York (SUNY) schools. Then we talk about the private schools.

Mrs. Estevez's future-oriented perspective involves sharing options for applying to a range of postsecondary institutions at the local, state, and private levels. In doing so, she supports students' and their families' choices about which colleges may best serve their needs.

Guidance Counselor Focus #2: Mr. Peretti (White). Mr. Peretti, a guidance counselor at Evergreen High School for more than 30 years, often starts conversations from students' own points of interest, and with humor, particularly when a student may not be sure about the type of career he or she wants to pursue.

I say, what's your career goal? Some of them really don't know. So then I ask them what they like, what they don't like. Do you want to be a mortician? That always gets them for some reason. No, I don't want to be a mortician. Well you don't know. Let's start with what you know. I go into colleges like that. It seems to satisfy everybody.

Similar to Mrs. Estevez, he begins conversations from students' current realities in terms of the learning environments in which they like or do not like to participate.

We start with whether they want to go here or whether they want to go away. And then the size, do you want a medium size school or do you want it smaller? How do you learn best? Do you learn with 50 people in your class, do you need one-on-one interaction with your teacher? . . . and then we talk about what they think they might want to do because that changes.

Both Mr. Peretti and Ms. Abrego utilize culturally relevant pedagogical practices by engaging students in college conversations as active participants in their college preparation. This future-oriented perspective and practice acknowledges students' present realities, builds on students' career and college choices, and takes into account families' cultural beliefs to move toward future opportunities. While studies based on affluent and middle class White students note the value of such practices, it is important to remember that working class Black and Latina/o students may not have had access to college visits or exposure to taken-for-granted college information (McDonough, 1997; Sacks, 2007). Moreover, culturally relevant future-oriented practices utilize students' cultural backgrounds to support their college readiness and access in under-resourced schools, especially where students and their families traditionally are viewed from deficit perspectives that tend to emphasize parental lack of involvement and educational goals for their children (Lipman, 1996; Valenzuela, 1999).

📖 **Reading in Action** 📖
1. What kind of futures do your students envision for themselves?
2. How can you engage a future-oriented perspective to support students' planning and decision making for college?
3. What are some further possibilities for engaging a future-oriented perspective with youth that considers their families' cultural beliefs?

(Un)Examined Norms: Facilitating or Hindering Students' Cultural Competence and Sociopolitical Consciousness

In addition to a future-oriented perspective some of the counselors use culturally relevant practices to highlight how their cultural background influences their practices and relationships with students. Excerpts from interviews with two guidance counselors at Evergreen High School demonstrate how their conversations with students revolve around their own experiences in college, their upbringing, and their understandings of urban students.

Guidance Counselor Focus #3: Ms. Johnson (Black). Ms. Johnson, who has worked at Evergreen High School for 3 years and who is pursuing graduate studies, uses her own college-going experiences to provide students with insight about the level of academic work that is needed to succeed in college.

> I give them my own experiences. I shove it down their throat. For instance, because I'm going for my master's, and I'm taking courses, the work I have, the level of work I learn or have to produce in my own courses, I show it to them. For instance, when they saw the book that I had to do for my term paper, I tell them, and I only ask you to do this. This is the real world. For those of you who think you're going to college, this is what is expected in college. . . . So I'm always showing— shoving the college experience down their throat. For me, what it was like when I first started college, when I went for my bachelor's. What it was like for me, and what is it like for me now, because I'm a different age group, doing different things and going back to school.

By focusing on her experiences, Ms. Johnson shares aspects of her development as a college student. She extends students' notions of college-going literacies by sharing expectations of herself as a student, specifically the work she has to produce, such as the term paper. For many students who may not have family members or peers who have attended college, Ms. Johnson provides an entry point for further conversations about developing a college-going identity.

Guidance Counselor Focus #4: Ms. Martin (White). Ms. Martin, a guidance counselor for 1 month, also helps students who live in an urban environment to grapple with the decision whether to live at home or to go away, based on her own experiences in college.

> I will encourage them to go away. I think it's such a once in a lifetime experience. To go away and study away from all of the associations of home. To be with all people your own age 24/7. And be challenged. I

think it is an experience many of us look back upon and say, "God, we'll never have this again. I'm so glad I was able to do this." I think it's very, very valid for our students.

A critical tenet of culturally relevant pedagogies is premised on understanding how a guidance counselor's cultural background influences and shapes his or her practices with Black and Latina/o students. Ms. Martin's expectation that going away to college is a realistic option for students is based on her own positive experiences of attending college. Yet, while Ms. Martin's experiences of going away provided a valuable experience for her, it is important to realize how students' cultural backgrounds and family values may collide with the value placed by counselors and teachers on going away to college. By not acknowledging existing cultural differences within and across racial ethnic groups, Ms. Martin misses an opportunity to explore the ways in which families' cultural beliefs around leaving home for college may signify different values within homes. For example, Gonzalez, Stoner, and Jovel (2003) demonstrated how in one study of 22 Latinas, researchers found many of the women felt their decision to leave home for college provided opportunities to develop their independence. Yet, the idea of going away to college was something new for many of the Latina families. It is important to support Latina youth to better understand the tensions and conflicts arising from a cultural value in which parents of Latinas struggle with the opportunities they want for their daughters, while at the same time wanting them to attend a local college close to home. For students of color, home and school cultures may represent potentially contradictory values, and the use of culturally relevant pedagogies offers one approach to support them. Furthermore, as guidance counselors, Ms. Johnson and Ms. Martin provide insight into ways educators may utilize culturally relevant practices to examine how their own cultural backgrounds and identities facilitate or support Latina/o and Black youth's educational experiences and college readiness and access.

GUIDANCE COUNSELORS AND TEACHERS: EXPLORING TENSIONS WITHIN PEDAGOGICAL PRACTICES

While the guidance counselors and teachers discussed thus far in this chapter provide examples of culturally relevant pedagogies that facilitate youth's college readiness and access, contradictions and tensions also exist in their practices. We highlight some of these contradictions and tensions by revisiting the practices of guidance counselors Mrs. Estevez and Mr. Peretti, pointing to the ways in which counselors may be operating along a continuum of culturally relevant practices that utilize students' cultures to support their learning and access to college. This continuum highlights the work involved in building upon students' cultural backgrounds to create and sustain a culturally relevant, schoolwide, college-going culture.

Mrs. Estevez (Latina, Guidance Counselor). Mrs. Estevez believes that the school's teachers and extracurricular clubs, such as ASPIRA, a national organization serving Latina/o youth, and the Asian Club, are addressing and affirming students' cultural identities in classes and the curriculum. Yet, her counseling practices do not emphasize the cultural identities of students but rather their family life. Her perceptions and expectations of students focus on them as individuals and, accordingly, include no special consideration for students' identities and culture. Mrs. Estevez feels that all kids are the same. However, she did note that she went "after outstanding students" and her "limited knowledge of students" made "it difficult to write recommendations" for students.

> Every kid is an individual. Personally, every kid is an individual to me and I work with them for who they are. It's not about what their culture is. I mean yes, I should . . . I mean . . . I understand the culture of the Latino and how parents don't want their kids to go away. You know the girls have to stay home. So we address those issues. So it's being sensitive to the students' backgrounds and finding out what family life is like. Because it's not just the Latino, I may have been an African American, I mean a Black girl whose mother doesn't want her to go either because she's overprotective. She wants her right there with her all the time. So it's a matter of just being open and sensitive to the kids, not so much background, but family life.

A focus on individuals can mask how culture plays a role in students' lives and their access to college. Some researchers would argue that Mrs. Estevez is operating from "cultural blindness . . . the belief that color and culture make no difference and that all people are the same" (Lindsey, Robins, & Terrell, 2009, p. 117). Surprisingly, Mrs. Estevez, who as part of her counseling responsibilities "treat[ed] students equally," in her former role as a teacher of Spanish engaged in several curricular and pedagogical practices that encouraged youth's college-going responsibilities. She noted that

> I've been a grade advisor for most of my years in Evergreen, because I worked with the ESL students for 9 years. I said what are you supposed to do in order to get your diploma? And within the Spanish class, we talked about careers, we talked about the future tense in grammar, so

we're talking about their future. We're talking about dreaming, with the conditional tense.

In addition to engaging a future-oriented perspective, she has high expectations for certain students. She notes, "From the Hispanics, I expect a little more, because they know what I'm saying all the time. The other kids struggle to understand what I'm saying, when I speak Spanish fluently." Mrs. Estevez's pedagogical practices supported students' multicultural college-going identities.

Mr. Peretti (White, Guidance Counselor). In the case of Mr. Peretti, he is very aware that his pedagogical style and his joy in being in a school with immigrant students are based on his own background.

> My grandfather came here from Italy. He had no money. He worked up. Then you see another generation move ahead. It's nice to see that. It's really interesting. I always tease them about their nationality and sometimes I think I cross the line. I want them to remember that they are special, unique. Not to forget. . . . It's a unique place. I feel very at home here, very comfortable.

He further notes:

> Most of the students [would be] first-generation college students . . . [who] just stare at you for a few minutes. You go back and tell them what you said again and then they understand. The motto is that everybody has to have at least some college. It doesn't matter. The bottom line is to make you healthy, wealthy, and wise. And that's by getting a job. That's the only way I know. That's what we stress.

As someone who comes from an immigrant background himself, Mr. Peretti finds himself comfortable in working with first- and second-generation college applicants. Because he is comfortable with students, he builds interpersonal relationships that affirm their identities as children of immigrants. He adopts a general philosophy that all students should go to college, reflecting his high expectations for students. Yet his interactions with first- and second-generation students do not build upon the strengths and needs of each generational group.

These excerpts from the guidance counselors reveal the contradictions and tensions embedded in their pedagogical counseling practices for Latina/o and Black youth. At times their different approaches to counselor–student relationships support students' educational experiences and college

readiness. For example, although some of the guidance counselors at Evergreen High School are adamant about treating the students as individuals, they simultaneously are declaring that all kids are the same. Moreover,
while they are supporting students' access to college-going opportunities,
the guidance counselors are disavowing the role and importance of ethnicity
and culture in their pedagogical counseling practices.

📖 Reading in Action 📖

1.   Consider Ms. Martin's and Ms. Johnson's culturally
relevant teaching practices and how you might
incorporate similar practices that build upon your
knowledge of students' cultures to support their college
readiness and access.
2.   In what ways does a focus on students as individuals
mask the role of culture in facilitating or hindering their
college readiness and access in your school?
3.   What tensions do you see arising in the ways
teachers, counselors, and administrators in your school
construct students' cultures?
4.   What kinds of prior experiences have enabled you
to understand and examine the ways in which your own
cultural background influences your culturally relevant
practices with students?

IMPLICATIONS AND CONCLUSION

Culturally relevant education that centers race, ethnicity, and culture reflects a respect for students', families' and staff's own cultural backgrounds,
which, in turn, influences the development of teachers' and counselors' policies and practices for Black and Latina/o youth. Specifically, cultural influences on teaching and learning play an important role in the creation of a
culturally relevant, schoolwide, educational environment in which strong
supportive relationships between school staff and youth are facilitated,
youth's college readiness is supported, and learning outcomes also include
the development of youth's personal, social, and political awareness of issues of college access. Culturally relevant educators move beyond an awareness of academic inequities for Black and Latina/o youth to enact beliefs
and practices that facilitate youth's academic achievement, cultural competence, and critical consciousness in preparing students to be college-ready
and apply to college. At the same time, there is an understanding that such
work is complicated and, at times, contradictory. Therefore, teachers and
counselors desiring to become culturally competent or to further develop

their cultural competencies can begin by examining how their own cultures have affected their educational process. For example, they can examine their PreK–20 educational experiences that were or were not culturally relevant, and deliberate as to why this might be so and how the cultural relevance of their experiences (or lack thereof) impacted their own educational, personal, social, and/or political outcomes. They also can examine how the dynamic between their own and the students' cultural backgrounds affects the policies and practices they enact to build on students' cultural backgrounds, identities, and assets to support their college readiness. The exemplary practices of the culturally relevant educators in this chapter reveal some of the teachers' and counselors' cultural competencies for improving youth educational experiences and facilitating more equitable and culturally relevant policies and practices.

TEACHER RESPONSE

A few weeks into my first year as an English teacher in an urban school, Thomas, a 9th-grade student of Caribbean descent, looked up from his desk and raised his hand. I expected a question about the Ernest J. Gaines text we were reading. Instead, he said, "Miss Marciano, what are you?" The question caught me off guard. I assumed my students knew I was White just by looking at me. I also assumed that the images of White middle class teachers prevalent in the media had taught the Black and Latina/o students with whom I worked more than they needed to know about the experiences of people like me. Rather than spend time sharing insight into my identity, I sought to learn about my students by asking them to write journal responses about their experiences as urban youth, and by talking with them about their lives and families. In attempting to engage students in the culturally relevant pedagogy I had read about in graduate school, and perhaps only superficially understood at the time, I focused my practice on students' cultural, ethnic, and linguistic identities and experiences rather than my own.

Yet, for Thomas and many of his classmates, who waited for my response that afternoon, "what I was" did matter. As students who had been instructed by teachers from a variety of racial and cultural backgrounds, including those who were Black, African, Latina/o, Caribbean, and Asian, many of the teenagers present in the classroom that day understood that my cultural experiences and theirs would impact our work together. For example, just because we were reading a text by Gaines, a Black author, focusing on the experiences of Black characters, didn't mean the Black students in my class would find the book compelling or relatable. In reflecting upon my own cultural identity, I realized that just because I was a White female teacher in an urban public school didn't mean that I hoped to be the Michelle Pfeiffer character in the popular film *Dangerous Minds* (Simpson & Bruckheimer, 1995), throwing candy bars at my students to get their attention. Although I answered Thomas's question with less agility than I'd care to admit, the conversation that ensued engaged more students than any previous class discussion we'd had in those first few weeks of school. And it began a dialogue about race and culture that continued throughout the school year as we tried to understand and overcome stereotypes about cultural groups, including those we identified with.

Now, more than a decade after Thomas raised his hand, I'm reminded of his question, particularly when thinking about the impact I and other teachers, guidance counselors, and administrators have on the college-going practices of Black and Latina/o urban youth and the development of their college-going identities. Often, for example, students want to know about my college experiences after they learn I attended a large university known for its basketball team. Early responses to such questions didn't take into account "what I was." I talked to students about the engaging classes I'd taken, the internships I completed, and what it was like to pledge a sorority, not recognizing the impact of my race and social class status on those experiences. Not only was I painting an unrealistic picture of what college was really like by focusing solely on the positive aspects of my experiences as a White woman at a predominantly White university, but I reinforced dominant culture stereotypes of what college is "supposed" to be as seen in popular media.

In current conversations about my college years, students and I discuss how our cultural backgrounds matter and consider how students' experiences as Black or Latina/o youth at the same college might be different. We talk, before and after class, as part of the curriculum, and at lunch time, about the academic and social challenges I faced as an undergraduate, highlighting the idea that just as my experiences don't necessarily fit into conventional perspectives of what it means to go college as shown in popular television programs such as *Gossip Girl* (McNally & Safran, 2008), neither will theirs. Rather, the richly diverse perspectives and identities students bring to each of their lived experiences also will impact their future encounters in college.

It may be easy for teachers, guidance counselors, and administrators of all racial and cultural backgrounds to perpetuate colorblind (Thompson, 1998) expectations of college going that position their own experience as the "norm," as I did during my initial conversations about college with students. In utilizing culturally relevant pedagogies, however, educators may cultivate interpersonal relationships that meet the college-going needs of youth (Siddle Walker & Tompkins, 2004). In doing so, expectations of the typical college experience as one toward which all youth should aspire may be overcome, supporting Black and Latina/o youth's access to college in the process.

An example of such a culturally relevant practice took place in my classroom recently when two of my former students and I discussed how we engaged in the college application process. I invited the students, who were seniors in college, to talk with my 12th-grade students about their experiences pursuing a college degree. The women, both Latina, were able to provide valuable insight from a perspective that I couldn't. For example, I experienced the normative college application process in which I applied to colleges in the fall and decided where to attend in the spring, informed by my parents' experiences as college graduates themselves. This traditional, linear process often is implicitly and explicitly reinforced by adults who work in schools and who have attended college themselves: Students who midway through senior year haven't yet applied to college often are viewed from a deficit perspective. The two young women who visited my classroom, however, described the more cyclical approach they took in applying to college, which resulted in their application and admission to a small private college a few weeks after their high school graduation, a process reflective of the needs of many Black and Latina/o youth who are often the first in their families to apply to college, or who are working in support of their families (Tierney, 2009). Many of the 12th-grade students in attendance that spring morning said they were encouraged by the former students' visit and excited to learn it wasn't too late for them to apply to colleges they hadn't considered previously.

As the preceding anecdote indicates, students benefit when school personnel create opportunities for authentic exchanges that build upon students' cultural experiences and challenge traditional structures of college-going processes that often are not reflective of the experiences of Black and Latina/o youth. When all who work with youth recognize that "what they are" matters in culturally relevant discussions of college-going, these exchanges have the potential to actively acknowledge the similarities and differences between the college-going experiences of adults and youth, creating further opportunities for students' cultures and identities to be utilized as sources of official knowledge.

Questions and Actions for Individuals

1. Describe the high school and college you attended. What were the cultural backgrounds of the students at these schools? How were cultural similarities and differences reflected in your experience at the schools? Were your experiences, including academic and social

interactions, reflective of all students at these schools? Why or why not?

2. When reading about the teachers and guidance counselors in the chapter, how were you reminded of your interactions as a high school student with school personnel? Would you consider the curriculum and teaching you encountered in high school to have been race-conscious or race-neutral? Why? In what ways did the curriculum and teaching reflect and build upon your race, ethnicity, and culture?

3. In your current interactions with youth, how do you engage in culturally relevant policies and practices that build on students' cultural backgrounds inclusive of race, ethnicity, and class? What tensions exist or may be created for you as you engage with youth in this way? How might you be supported within your school context to further engage in culturally relevant policies and practices?

Questions and Actions for Small Groups Within School Communities

1. Describe some examples of culturally relevant policies and practices within your school. Where, when, and by whom do these policies and practices occur? Which students do they serve?

2. Consider the opportunities that are present to connect your policies and practices to students' cultural, ethnic, and linguistic identities and experiences. When and how are such opportunities created?

3. What resources exist for building upon students' cultural, ethnic, and linguistic identities and experiences within the school to support youth's college readiness and access?

Questions and Actions for Whole-School Communities

1. Consider the schoolwide policies and practices relating to the college-going process enacted by teachers, guidance counselors, and administrators in your school. What are some examples of culturally relevant policies and practices? How do such practices build upon students' cultural strengths and academic successes while supporting their college-going identities? What opportunities exist to further support the cultural, academic, and college-going identities of youth?

2. Discuss the schoolwide policies and practices that impact the information about college that students receive. Is the information students receive reflective of their cultural, ethnic, and linguistic identities and experiences? Why or why not?

3. What opportunities exist for students to gather information about college going from people with racial or ethnic identities similar to and different from their own? How might such opportunities assist students in developing their own college-bound identities?

CHAPTER 4

Creating Possibilities

Black Males' and Latinos' (Non-) Successful Negotiations of High-Stakes Testing and Extracurricular Activities

with Hui Soo Chae

I heard a lot of people talking about [this school] and they wanted to go to it, and I heard my teacher saying it's like one of the best schools in the whole city. . . . [It] was my first choice. . . . [In the future] I see myself being a journalist.

—Gary, Black, male student

I've got good grades. I want to play baseball . . . the people who say they're going to junior college, I'm like, no way, I'm going to a four-year, and I'm going to go away. Some of them, they don't have the choice to go away, their grades aren't good enough. They're going to have to go to community colleges.

—Andre, Latino, student

I'm not too comfortable with Regents. It's counterproductive in my opinion. It has the students on edge every end of January and June for a test that they may not even use because they're going to school out of state. I went to school in Pennsylvania—they didn't care if I had the Regents or not. They just knew that I had graduated with x-amount of classes and what my average was in that class, but they didn't look at my Regents. . . . Now [students] have to pass x-amount of Regents in order to graduate. That's another bias . . . not everybody's a good test-taker, even though they might be a good student in the classroom.

—Ms. Samuels, White, teacher

It always helps to have an extracurricular activity on the college application, even if it's just a club. It may not be for a sports scholarship or academic scholarship but this shows the colleges that you at least participated at the school. It helps that borderline student. They may look at that as an incentive for you to do well, or you had the drive to at least participate.

—Mr. Steele, Black, special education teacher and coach

We recently presented to teachers, teacher educators, and graduate students popular media images of high school students from television shows and movies such as *Glee* (Falchuk & Buecker, 2010), *Dangerous Minds* (Simpson & Bruckheimer, 1995), *Gossip Girl* (McNally & Safran, 2008), and *College Hill Atlanta* (Edmonds, 2008), and asked them to share how they think Latino and Black male students are represented within these shows. They stated that Latinos and Black males were either missing, portrayed as middle class and acting like the White students, or shown as adolescents who are in constant trouble and apathetic toward their education (Casillas, 2012; Trier, 2005). Yet, Andre, Gary, and their teachers/coaches in the excerpts above provide insight into a range of complex experiences that illustrate how Latinos and Black males negotiate the overlapping and intersecting influences and experiences of academic choice and preparation, cultural identities, and extracurricular activities as aspiring college-bound youth. Their perspectives are increasingly important in facilitating understandings of how educators can support youth's academic learning, cultural identities, and sociopolitical awareness as engaged citizens amid what many educators have deemed a "crisis" of education for Latinos and Black males. Specifically, Tyrone Howard (2010) argues that the "underachievement and disenfranchisement [of Black males] in schools and society seem to be reaching pandemic and life threatening proportions" (p. 956). This crisis has been documented through tremendous racial and gender disparities in graduation rates and college attendance rates for youth in the United States, as shown in Appendix A. The Editorial Projects in Education Research Center (2011) reported 2009 nationwide graduation rates for Asian males at 79.2%, Black males at 51.9%, Latinos at 58.1%, and White males at 76.1%. Additionally, a systemic gender gap in the graduation rates of male and female students exists. Nationwide, the graduation rate for Black males was 13.4% lower than the rate for Black female students (65.3%). Similarly, the national graduation rate for Latinos was 8% lower than the rate for Latinas (66.1%). In New York State, the graduation rates for Latinos and Black males were 53.3% for both, compared with 61.2% for Latinas and 61% for Black female students. In creating a culturally relevant high school college-going culture responsive to the aspirations and needs of Latinos and Black males, we argue that it is imperative that educators and family members understand how these youth negotiate their daily experiences and what they say is working (or not) for them as they pursue admission to a college.

In this chapter, we focus on 11 working class Latinos and Black males in our study who emerge as either "successful" or "(non-)successful negotiators" of institutional structures, and some of their teachers', counselors', and administrators' perspectives of who and what is influencing their college-going processes. We draw attention to the academic preparation provided within the school and school-sponsored extracurricular activities—particularly sports teams—which were cited by youth as two primary reasons they attended Evergreen High School. Researchers have shown how these two school structures serve to enhance or hinder experiences in high school, school connections, and success for ethnically diverse students' educational experiences, particularly those of Black males and Latinos (Brown & Evans, 2002; Guest & Schneider, 2003; Holloway, 2002; Jordan & Cooper, 2003; Noguera, Hurtado, & Fergus, 2012). However, little research has demonstrated how college readiness is influenced by culturally relevant curriculum and the relationships among youth, peers, teachers, and counselors. We raise questions about how culturally relevant curriculum and teaching that acknowledge and build upon the cultural knowledge, beliefs, and practices Latinos and Black males bring to school further support their academic learning, cultural competencies, and sociopolitical awareness to facilitate more equitable access to college.

With the increasing use of state exams as requirements for high school graduation, educators are critiquing education policies by examining how factors such as race, class, gender, and (dis)ability impact student achievement on these exams. Advocates of high-stakes testing argue that such accountability systems lead to more equitable school structures that support all students' cultural and academic identities regardless of race, class, (dis)ability, or English proficiency. Yet, large-scale quantitative analyses show that these exams have a disproportionately negative impact on Black males and Latino youth (Horn, 2003; Orfield & Kornhaber, 2001). For example, Natriello and Pallas (2001), providing an account of the negative consequences of high-stakes testing, write that high-stakes testing decreases the likelihood that minority and poor students will graduate from high school, thereby limiting their access to a broad range of postsecondary education options. We take their findings a step further, utilizing qualitative research to examine Black male and Latino students' daily negotiations of their intersecting cultural and academic identities and the New York State Regents exams, as shown in Table 4.1.

Moreover, extracurricular activities at the high school level, such as sports, performing-arts groups, and student government, are heralded as

Table 4.1. Youth Participants' Background and Testing Profile (9th–12th Grades)

Student Name	Successful Negotiator	Race/National Background	Family's Generation U.S. Status	(Dis)ability School-Identified	Track Within House	School Extracurricular Participation	English (65)	Math (55)	Science (55)	Global History (65)	U.S. History (65)	Total Pass/Fail
Gary	Yes	Black Ghanaian	First	No	Honors Health	Yes	P	P	P	P	P	5/0
Andre	Yes	Latino Dominican	First	No	Honors Health	Yes	P	P	P	P	P	5/0
Abraham	Yes	Black Nigerian	First	No	Honors Health	Yes	P	P	P	P	P	5/0
Damon	Yes	Black Jamaican	First	No	Honors Health	Yes	P	P	P	P	P	5/0
Derek	No	Black	Third+	Yes	Health	No	F	F	F	F	F	0/5
Dante	No	Black Jamaican	First	Yes	General	No	F	F	P	P	F	2/3
Jason	No	Black Jamaican	First	Yes	General	No	P	P	F	F	F	2/3
Dillon	No	Black	Third+	No	Health	No	F	F	F	F	F	0/5
Jorge	No	Latino Puerto Rican	First	No	General	No	F	F	F	F	F	0/5
Juan	No	Latino Puerto Rican	First	No	General	No	P	P	P	F	F	2/3
Jesus	No	Latino Dominican	First	No	Health	No	P	F	P	P	F	3/2

institutional structures that positively impact and affirm students' cultural and academic identities, engagement in schools, academic achievement, educational aspirations, and future educational attainment (Holland & Andre, 1987; Tierney & Colyar, 2005). With colleges and universities becoming increasingly selective and calling for applicants to develop a talent and show depth of commitment to a few activities, early involvement in extracurricular activities is imperative in order for Black and Latina/o youth from under-resourced urban communities to be competitive applicants for college. McDonough (1997) describes the competitiveness of college access, manifested by applicants whose economic status enables them to hire private consultants to help in the application process. For working class Black male and Latino youth who do not have access to such resources, acquisition of experiences and skills needed to compete in the college application process is facilitated by mentoring in cross-age peer groups and by teachers/coaches in extracurricular structures (Marsh & Kleitman, 2002; Quiroz, 2000).

📖 Reading in Action 📖

1. Refer to the quotes at the beginning of this chapter and consider how they reflect your understandings of youth's college-going aspirations and ideas about the role of graduation exams and extracurricular activities in schools.
2. What images of Latinos and Black males and education do you see represented in the media? How do these images connect (or not) to the prevailing images of males in your school? What opportunities are there for youth to respond to and critique these images?
3. What state exams and extracurricular activities are offered for the youth with whom you work? How do the testing and extracurricular structures support or limit youth's college readiness and career futures while building upon their cultural backgrounds, identities, and perspectives?

"SUCCESSFUL NEGOTIATORS": INSTITUTIONAL STRUCTURES SUPPORTING LATINOS AND BLACK MALES

In the following section, we highlight the experiences and perspectives of four working class Latinos and Black males, Abraham, Andre, Damon, and Gary. We define these students as "successful negotiators" of their high school educational experiences and institutional beneficiaries of the school's culturally relevant policies and practices. Their engagement provided learning opportunities that reinforced both their cultural and their academic identities as they prepared to successfully pass the state exams and aspired to attend college. These four students were accepted by state or private liberal arts colleges.

Intersecting Academic and Cultural Identities

Abraham, Andre, Damon, and Gary successfully completed all their state exam requirements before the end of their senior year, participated in extracurricular activities, graduated from high school within 4 years, and were admitted to colleges of their choice. In focusing on these youth's successes, we move beyond a focus on failure for Latinos and Black males. Highlighting the practices of "successful negotiators" provides significant insight into understanding the complex intersecting identities of Black males and Latinos, the curricular and extracurricular school structures supportive of their cultural and academic identities, and their negotiations of graduation exams.

Gary, who was born in Ghana, is fluent in Twi and an active member of the Evergreen High School community. His senior year has been busy because of his Advanced Placement English class. He will attend Saint Peter's College to pursue a career in journalism. Abraham, whose family is made up of first-generation immigrants from Nigeria, will enroll at State University of New York (SUNY) Geneseo to study nursing. He is fluent in Igbo and participates in several activities in and out of school. Damon was born in Jamaica and immigrated to the United States with his family when he was a child. He describes Evergreen as "the best school in the New York City" because it has many opportunities and activities for students. On weekdays he is involved in various sports and/or school-sponsored activities. For the past 2 years, he has worked as a golf caddy on weekends. He will attend one of the SUNY colleges. Andre's family is made up of first-generation immigrants from the Dominican Republic. He was born in New York and is fluent in Spanish. During his freshman year, he was on the track team from September to February and on the baseball team from March to August. He is recognized as one of the best players on the baseball team and hopes to play in college. He will attend SUNY Stony Brook.

The patterns of academic achievement among the three 1.5/second-generation, Black immigrant, male students (Gary, Abraham, Damon) build on research that finds first- and second-generation African and Caribbean youth have higher high school graduation rates than students who are third-plus generation (Rong & Brown, 2001; Waters, 1999). According to this research, Black immigrant youth tend to emphasize their ethnic or national identities rather than a Black identity, which allows them to distance themselves from African American youth whom they perceive to be low achievers academically.

Yet even as youth construct their ethnic and national identities, Gary and Abraham recognize that their teachers construct them as Black. Abraham stated, "Basically, nobody believes I'm African. They always say you don't look like [an African]. But I really don't care. I was born here [but] my background is still African." Gary also challenges fixed, essentialized notions of a single racial/ethnic identity by further self-identifying as Ghanaian, Twi-speaking, and the captain of the school soccer team (Allen, Jackson, & Knight, 2012). Damon, who identifies as Jamaican in the context of his participation in the school's extracurricular Caribbean Club, also identifies as Black in contexts such as the Evergreen Black History Show. These young men are aware of how race is shaping how they are viewed by their teachers (Howard, 2010). Moreover, the shifting between an ethnic and a racial identity challenges research by Waters (1999) and Rong and Brown (2001), who write that Black immigrant youth are often forced to choose between an ethnic immigrant identity and the identity of being a Black American. By better understanding the ways in which Black males and Latinos identify their multiple and shifting cultural, racial, national, and ethnic identities, school personnel may be able to better provide culturally relevant policies and practices to support these youth.

The extracurricular structures at Evergreen High School appeared to support Andre's academic and cultural identities. Specifically, Andre was one of the highest achieving students in our study. Andre does not perceive a conflict between his ethnicity and academic success. He says, "[I am able to express my identity] in school by getting good grades. I'm getting popular because of sports. . . . If I weren't Dominican, I probably would not be playing baseball . . . because over there they play baseball a lot." The literature on Latino youth's school achievement suggests that Andre's academic "success" in passing all five of his required state exams is more the exception than the norm. According to these studies, Latinos often experience difficulty in school because of conflicts between the cultures of the home and school (Valenzuela, 1999). Specifically, since schools often do not value the cultural backgrounds of Latino youth, they frequently devalue their cultural identities, thereby perpetuating unsupportive school structures and classroom practices. Insight into Abraham's, Andre's, Damon's, and Gary's cultural and academic identities reveals that although identities can be imposed, individuals also have agency to define their cultural identities. Moreover, their perspectives allow educators to see the ways in which they do not necessarily construct their identities in opposition to the "mainstream" or adopt an oppositional culture.

Intersecting Identities and Curricular and Pedagogical Practices

Understanding the intersections of youth's multiple cultural and academic identities and their negotiations of exams required for high school graduation also provides a more in-depth understanding of the school structures that facilitate youth's success (Knight, 2003). Abraham, Andre, Damon, and Gary, who had completed all the high school testing requirements, asserted academic identities connected to the honors/college-bound classes they had been tracked into. According to these students, their academic identities were supported by teachers whom they believed were well prepared, supportive, and adequately preparing them for the Regents. Damon remarked, "[My teachers] tell us everything we [can] expect on the Regents. [They] tell us how it is going to be . . . [and they] give us a few Regents questions that they think might be put on the Regents."

These students shared that their teachers spent a considerable amount of time preparing students for NYS Regents Examinations. Specifically, they commented that classroom activities were relevant to the content being tested on the Regents exams. Gary stated, "Just last period I took a U.S. history test. It was the same questions from this January Regents . . . the same thing. So I think you get familiar with the kind of question you gonna see on the Regents. 'Cause the Regents it might be the same question but it could be asked in a different way." Although they criticized the methods used for exam preparation (e.g., cramming, weekly reviews), they believed these methods played a key role in their success on the exams. Abraham shared that "Mr. Thomas [his U.S. history teacher] gave us questions from the Regents review book starting Day 1. It was mad boring. . . . But I think everyone in the class passed. No one I know failed." Similarly, Andre noted, "[The math teacher] has some tests that are strictly Regents questions that she doesn't count toward your [class] grade. . . . She looks at the grade [and which] one of the answers are [most often incorrect], and then she would reuse the [question]. Then she collects it again like a little quiz to see if you got better. And she just keeps retesting us with different questions."

The significance of these findings for the four working class Black male and Latino youth should not be underestimated. They provide insights into the school structures, specifically classroom practices, that support youth's academic identities and their academic preparation and aspirations to attend college. Moreover, these findings confirm literature that reports teachers in higher tracks "are clearer, more enthusiastic, and use less strong criticism and classroom learning tasks appear to be better organized and of greater variety" (Oakes, 1987, p. 142). When students have access to teachers who value some aspect of youth's multiple identities (in this case, students' academic identities), classroom practices and instructional strategies are more likely to support student learning, thereby improving the likelihood for student success on state exams. Although curricular and pedagogical practices within some of their courses supported youth's academic identities, these practices did not recognize the cultural identities of Black and Latino working class youth. For instance, several youth commented that what they learned in their classes did not reflect any of their lived experiences. Youth's understandings of the necessity for cultural relevancy in the curriculum should not be discounted. Unfortunately, the heterogeneity of Black male experiences remained invisible, and opportunities to provide culturally relevant educational experiences were lost. This invisibility begs the question of whether the young men would have scored significantly higher on the exams and entered more selective colleges that "fit" their aspirations if the curriculum had supported a healthy racial-ethnic identity and one that was more meaningful and culturally relevant (Howard, 2010; Wright, 2011).

📖 Reading in Action 📖

1. What are some of the ways in which you may further your understanding of the cultural backgrounds, interests, and experiences of Black male and Latino students?
2. How might you incorporate youth's perceptions of what works for them academically into policies and practices you enact to prepare them for required state exams?
3. Youth are enacting practices of negotiating and analyzing in their daily practices outside of school. In what ways can you build upon these practices to support youth in meeting learning standards that call for them to demonstrate these skills?

Culturally Relevant Pedagogy Within Extracurricular Activities

In addition to facilitating academic excellence, culturally relevant education policies and practices facilitate students' social, cultural, and psychological well-being (Ladson-Billings, 1995). The high-achieving males found such support in the extracurricular activities offered at the school, which touted having 60 clubs and extracurricular activities. Andre, Abraham, Damon, and Gary were engaged in at least one extracurricular school activity for 3 or more years. Andre has played baseball at Evergreen since 9th grade and plays in various leagues out of school in the off-season. Similarly,

Damon has been a member of the school track team since 9th grade and participates in school organizations and events like the Caribbean Club and the Evergreen Talent Show. Meanwhile, Gary, a member of the school soccer team for 3 years and team captain during his senior year, recognized the connection between extracurricular activities and college admissions, encouraging his friend Abraham to join a sports team to improve his chances of attending college. Based on Gary's advice, Abraham participated in the school volleyball team for 3 years and was a volunteer in the principal's office during his senior year. Andre, Abraham, Damon, and Gary all seemed well aware of the connection between participating in extracurricular activities and college going that supported their cultural and academic identities (Tierney, Corwin, & Colyar, 2005; Welch & Hodges, 1997).

These students remarked several times during informal conversations that these extracurricular activities were popular among youth of their ethnic background and supportive of their cultural identities. For instance, Gary stated that it was common for Ghanaian, Nigerian, and other African immigrant youth to try out for the school soccer team because of the popularity of the sport in the countries they emigrated from. Similarly, Andre believed that the popularity of baseball in Caribbean nations such as the Dominican Republic and Puerto Rico was the reason the school baseball team was predominantly Latino. Although these comments may perpetuate particular stereotypes about the types of sports African and Caribbean immigrants excel in, it is important to note that these young men believed these sports activities were compatible with their cultural identities and interests (Flores-Gonzalez, 2002).

Andre, Abraham, Damon, and Gary also shared that these school-sponsored activities, and in particular coaches and peers on the sports teams, supported their academic learning and were an important source of information about high school graduation exams, SAT tests, college applications, and financial aid. A cultural norm existed on these teams whereby students interacted with and learned from older, more experienced teammates. Andre says, "I might talk to a kid from track or baseball, and be like, how [did] you get into college, what did you score on your SAT and stuff?" Such questioning helps Andre to develop an understanding of what steps he needs to take in order to attend college. Gary also adds that "a guy on the soccer team . . . was writing his essay. He got another [student] who was a senior in this school [and] they went to the learning center every day after . . . 'cause they were helping you write your essay . . . [and] other students helping other students with their essays." Gary took seriously his responsibility to share with his teammates information about graduating from high school and preparing for college. His responsibility resonated with a sense of "collective struggle" in preparing his teammates for the state exams and SAT as others had prepared him (O'Connor, 1999; Tierney & Hagedorn, 2002). Although some researchers note that Black and Latino youth are more vulnerable to negative peer pressure (Rong & Brown, 2001), the "successful negotiators" used peer networks as a way to academically support their friends. For example, Gary supported Abraham academically by assisting him with schoolwork and providing him with information about tutoring sessions and school-based SAT help. The peer relationship that Gary shared with Abraham was common among the "successful negotiators."

Coaches and extracurricular advisors also played a key institutional role in helping male participants understand and negotiate the various requirements for high school graduation, college admissions, and college athletics eligibility. Mr. Bard, a gym teacher and coach, noted:

> I ask them what's your interest in college, are you interested in going to college, are you interested in going to run [track], and once they say they are we go through a process, we discuss financial aid forms, we're always discussing SATs, the importance of it and grades. Certain forms come from the colleges. They fill it out, they bring it back to me, we go over it together, and whatever needs to be changed, then I send it out. . . . Now, it's up to them if they want to go or not. Let them know that it's important to go to college. Especially for our kids . . . our minority kids.

Similarly, Mr. Steele, a special education teacher and coach, shared about the types of conversations he has with his team and students:

> I'm preaching all the time about college. Conversations have included what sort of college to go to; what's right for me? Do I need to go to a two-year school or a four-year school? What makes one better than the other? Out-of-state school as compared to in-state school; will I get a scholarship? Things of that nature would be in conversations I have all the time. What school did I go to?

Within extracurricular activities, especially sports, Black and Latino male youth are gaining access to valuable resources and knowledge preparing them for college. These coaches and advisors exemplify Shuford's (1998) notion of the "educator-coach," a person whose increased contact with student athletes places him or her in a position to take responsibility for supporting youth's cultural and academic identities by assisting them to negotiate high school graduation and how to choose a college that will be a good fit for them. These culturally relevant conversations and interactions provided youth with access to information about college admissions, financial aid, preparation for college, and varied understandings of the types of college choices available.

📖 Reading in Action 📖

1. How do the extracurricular activities offered at your school play a role in Black males' and Latinos' successful negotiation of high school and enrollment in college?
2. In what ways do the extracurricular activities offered at your school support the academic and cultural backgrounds and experiences of Black males and Latinos? How might more opportunities for such activities be developed or maintained within your school?
3. In what ways have you seen the relationships coaches, advisors, and students develop while participating in extracurricular activities support youth's college readiness and access?

"(NON-)SUCCESSFUL NEGOTIATORS": INSTITUTIONAL STRUCTURES INADEQUATELY SUPPORTING YOUTH'S IDENTITIES

Some Latino and Black male students were positioned as "(non-)successful negotiators" through school policies and practices that did not adequately support their academic and cultural identities. Specifically, seven immigrant and non-immigrant Black males and Latinos, Dillon, Derek, Dante, Jason, Juan, Jesus, and Jorge, did not pass the state exams required for high school graduation. We refer to these students as "non-successful negotiators" in the context of two institutional policies and practices that did not adequately support their cultural and academic identities. These include (1) insufficient preparation for success on the state exams, leading to the placement of youth in a systemic "re-tracking structure," and (2) non-involvement in school-sponsored activities. These men represent a diverse range of intersecting cultural and academic backgrounds and identities. For instance, among the four Black males, Dante and Jason are second-generation Caribbean immigrants, while Derek and Dillon come from families that have lived in the United States for more than three generations. For three of the four Black males (Dante, Jason, and Derek), "learning disabled," a school classification, is an identity that intersects with their ethnicity and generational status. All three of the Latinos, Juan, Jesus, and Jorge, come from families that are first-generation immigrants. All the "non-successful" Black males and Latinos were in the "regular" (non-honors) tracks within the school. Although they were involved in activities within their communities, few were involved in school-sponsored extracurricular activities. The findings reveal that these males did not become institutional beneficiaries of a schoolwide culture that fostered culturally relevant policies and practices.

Intersecting Academic and Cultural Identities

The intersecting cultural identities that were most significant to the three Latinos were ethnicity, generational status, and fluency in Spanish. Jesus, who was born in the Dominican Republic, is fluent in Spanish. He describes Evergreen as a school with a good reputation, but is not involved in the school's extracurricular activities. He spends his free time with a close network of Latino friends playing basketball and video games. Juan, who identifies as Puerto Rican, was born in New York City and also is fluent in Spanish. He was a member of the school ROTC Club in 9th grade but left because it was "not fun anymore." He hopes to attend the Air Force Academy. Jorge, who was born in the United States, is Puerto Rican and speaks some Spanish. He asserted that he "wouldn't be Puerto Rican if he didn't know how to speak Spanish." Outside of school he regularly plays basketball at a local community center and volunteers as a tutor at an elementary school. He wants to go to college so that he can be one of the people in his family who "gets the chance to succeed."

Race, ethnicity, generational status, and learning (dis)ability were intersecting cultural identities frequently cited among the four Black males. Dillon, whose family has lived in the United States for several generations, identifies himself as Black. He hopes to become a math teacher once he finishes college. For the past 2 years, he has worked as a supermarket cashier. Similarly, Derek comes from a family that has lived in the United States for more than three generations and identifies strongly with a Black racial identity. He loves music and hopes to pursue a career in the performing arts. He plays several instruments and is a member of his church choir. According to Derek, "learning disabled" (LD) is a significant identity that intersects with his Black identity in school. He explains that being "LD" helped him form friendships with other students labeled "LD" in the school. Yet, being labeled as "LD" often means students are segregated from their peers, and may not be perceived by school personnel as college bound (Reid & Knight, 2006). Dante, whose family immigrated to the United States from Jamaica when he was a child, identifies as Jamaican. He describes himself as a "bad kid" who is trying to do the right thing. Going to college is not that important to him. He believes that college is a "money-making" industry and that he can do well in life with only a high school diploma. Like Derek, Dante receives special services (e.g., resource teacher) in school because he is labeled "LD." Jason, who also describes himself as Jamaican, comes from a family that immigrated to the United States from England. He said that the only person he talks to about college is his older cousin, who previously attended Evergreen. Like Derek and Dante, Jason recognizes that his "LD" identity significantly influences the education he receives in school.

The recognition of students' various intersecting identities is critical to developing practices and policies that are supportive of Black males' and Latinos' academic achievement (De Gaetano, Williams, & Volk, 1998; Knight & Oesterreich, 2002). For instance, Black youth who are also recent immigrants to the United States may not receive English language services in school if teachers and administrators believe that these students are African Americans, and thus are unaware of their linguistic needs. According to our participants ("successful" and "non-successful negotiators"), teachers and administrators at Evergreen are unaware of their intersecting cultural identities. For example, Dillon states, "I don't think I am able to express my cultural identity." When asked, "Would you say there is anyone in this school who supports you as an African American male?" he emphatically says, "No."

Further comments made by these youth also reflect the separation between their cultural identities, school experiences, and state exams. For instance, although the seven youth knew they had to pass five state exams to graduate from high school, they did not know how the exams impacted their educational experiences and their opportunities to pursue postsecondary education. Two participants, Dillon and Jason, commented at the end of 10th grade that they still knew "nothing" about the Regents, whereas Jason knew only that his friends "got burned on the tests." He went on to say, "[I know] nothing about Regents exams . . . I know it's hard. . . . My friends . . . say you have to study, like 24 hours. I said, 'I can't study that long.' . . . [The school] says you've got to pass the Regents." When school communities are unaware of the complexities resulting from youth's intersecting identities, teachers, counselors, and administrators miss important opportunities to develop meaningful relationships with youth. Without these relationships, students lose access to critical information about state exams, high school graduation requirements, and the college-going process, and thus may not understand the connection between state exams and college admissions.

At the same time it is important to acknowledge that what little these students do know about the Regents comes from their teachers. Jorge stated, "Well, the teachers I have tell me about [the Regents]—it scares me a little. They say if you don't do your work you are going to be in for it because they give you 2 years' worth of work on your Regents." Jason also acknowledged that his resource teacher "is always there for [him] . . . he always helps me. . . . When I don't understand the work, he always helps me, no matter what class it's in. . . . [I see him] five periods a week." The perspectives of these males and their critique of school structures afford teachers opportunities to understand how they can support youth's academic and cultural identities as they interact with students daily.

📖 **Reading in Action** 📖
1. How might you be supported in understanding the cultural backgrounds and identities of the youth with whom you work? In what ways can you use these understandings to strengthen their academic identities?   2. How have you seen Black male and Latino students disadvantaged by school structures that do not support their cultural and academic identities?   3. In what ways can resource teachers and content area teachers collaborate to provide the academic and cultural support Black males and Latinos need to successfully negotiate their learning experiences?

Intersecting Identities and Curricular and Pedagogical Practices

In addition to discussing the culturally relevant policies and practices needed to support their academic and cultural identities, these seven males offered a critique of their preparation for the state exams, highlighting how they were positioned to not successfully pass them. These critiques were supported by some, such as Ms. Samuels in the opening excerpt of the chapter, in regard to the importance of and preparation for high school graduation exams. Specifically, the Latinos and Black males believed that their teachers and classes were insufficiently preparing them for success on the state exams, leading to their failure and subsequent "re-tracking" into remedial classes. They were concerned that their classwork was not connected to the content of the state exams, and that classroom time was spent inappropriately, working on projects, watching movies, and reviewing material that did not appear on state exams. These practices are emblematic of a system of instructional inequality that hinders student negotiations and achievement on state exams and high school graduation. Some students believed that their teachers were hard to understand, unknowledgeable about their subject area, impatient, boring, and off-topic.

My earth science teacher, she doesn't teach us nothing. Like, she will sit there, and write on the board, and just stay quiet. The whole class will talk, and she wouldn't care. You could walk out of the class, and not come back, and it won't matter. . . . She will not ask where you're going, try to stop you or anything. Students from other classes, they'll go into the class and just stay there. And people will just walk in the door, scream, and she wouldn't care. So going to her class is like a waste of time for me. (Jesus, Latino, student)

According to research literature, one possible explanation for teachers' inadequate performance is their difficulty in preparing appropriate instructional activities in high-stakes environments.

These youth also shared stories of teachers who reviewed state exam material the week before the exam, or teachers who told them they were responsible for attending review classes after school or on Saturdays. Students who attend are given incentives in the form of extra credit points on the final course grade. However, none of Latinos or Black males, both the "non-successful" and the "successful negotiators," were able to attend these review sessions consistently because of work schedules, extracurricular commitments, and personal obligations to family and friends. Although students in the honors sections were unable to attend the sessions, the consequences were less significant for them, as they received support from teachers, coaches, and peers in school. Conversely, non-successful students had few school structures they could utilize to receive further academic support in passing state exams. This further underscores the importance of scheduling multiple exam review sessions at times that are sensitive to the lives of working class Black male and Latino youth.

The lack of curricular and pedagogical support for preparing youth to take state exams, and the absence of school structures (e.g., review sessions) that recognize youth's multiple identities, contributed to student failure on these exams, causing students in the regular sections to become part of a systemic "re-tracking structure." This structure exacerbates initial differences between students and widens the achievement gap between students in the high and low tracks (Oakes, Wells, & Jones, 1997). For instance, students who fail a state exam become part of a cycle that maintains their placement in the same courses, reinforcing the perception among teachers of their low ability levels. This system of "re-tracking" is particularly significant because it hinders students' academic progress, limiting their opportunities to take other courses that could improve their chances for college admissions. A few students added that retaking courses to pass state exams did not allow them to take a higher level English class to prepare for the SAT. Missing this class has a significant impact on youth's negotiations of their college preparation efforts, particularly for those students unable to obtain SAT preparation outside of school.

📖 **Reading in Action** 📖
1. How might you reflect upon youth's academic and cultural identities to ensure your practices consider the intricacies of youth's daily lives?
2. In what ways have you seen failure to pass a state exam lead to other negative academic consequences for students in schools (e.g., the narrowing of course selection)?
3. How do you offer opportunities for Black males and Latinos to critique what is working (or not) for them to assist in your creation of culturally relevant policies and practices that prepare them to attend college?

A Lack of Culturally Relevant Pedagogy Within Extracurricular Activities

Another significant theme highlighting the experiences of Black males and Latinos was their involvement in extracurricular school activities. Similar to the students in the honors classes, Dillon, Derek, Dante, Jason, Juan, Jesus, and Jorge attended Evergreen because of its academic and extracurricular offerings. Jorge remarked, "I put [Evergreen] as my first choice high school. I heard that it was a great academic school, [and] I always wanted a great sports school." However, they had little to no involvement in the school-sponsored extracurricular activities. School officials and these youth provided several explanations for their lack of participation. The majority of the club advisors, teachers, and administrators with whom we spoke regarded the absence of 9th-grade students as a natural phenomenon within the school. The explanation of Ms. Smith, the music teacher, which mirrored those of other club advisors and coaches, was that 9th-graders are "still getting used to the school." However, beyond 9th grade there was a gendered cultural norm that hindered Black male and Latino youth's access to extracurricular activities (Lopez, 2002). Although there were sports teams for both males and females, males were largely absent from clubs, particularly in leadership positions. Mr. Vern, the director of extracurricular activities, explained this phenomenon away: "If you look at all the clubs, it's mostly girls. Student leadership meetings; it's all girls. Senior counsel is girls. The guys are weak." This dismissal of males was also evident in the words of Ms. Frank, the nature club sponsor, who stated, "You know, you can't just say I'm going to make sure I get a male in here. I can't do that. I don't have the—we don't have the time to dedicate to this, to make sure there's male structure in here."

In addition to the lack of gendered support for Latinos and Black males, some of the youth's reasons for non-involvement reveal the complexities of their intersecting identities and daily lives that they are negotiating in and out of school. For example, several structural limitations within schools, such as limited slots for varsity sports participation and uninteresting activities, did not encourage their participation. Further, some youth noted that institutional structures (e.g., bulletin boards, the school newspaper, teachers) failed to provide information about the existence and beginning date of activities, contributing to their non-involvement. In some cases, youth missed the day of tryouts for some of the sports teams. Consequently, they were excluded from activities they considered compatible with their cultural identities. In almost every case, youth who did not make their team of choice were unable to find another activity that supported their cultural identity and was of interest to them.

> Since my freshman year, [my counselors] have been telling me [to join extracurricular activities], but in the school, I don't find any extracurricular activities . . . really interesting. I don't think there is any in this school. . . . It would have to be something that would keep you occupied . . . something physical . . . I could play sports all day. (Jesus, Latino, student)

Although these students were not participating in school-sponsored activities, they were involved in community activities and/or work responsibilities that were connected to their identities. They included jobs, church choir, theatre groups, modeling, sports teams, cello lessons, and familial commitments. For Dillon, the primary activity was work. "[My] main reason [for working is] my parents. . . . I feel I should do stuff for my family. . . . I think I owe them, like 17 years of the same thing." Jorge was involved with tutoring in an after-school program and was being recognized by the borough president for his service. Additionally, he attended a program on Saturdays that allowed him to practice singing and dancing. This provided him with an opportunity to perform on the Disney Channel. However, it is significant to note that these forms of participation were not recognized within school (Scribner & Reyes, 1999). As a result, student participation in activities outside of school was not seen as valuable or relevant to the academic success of these youth.

These perspectives also reveal that extracurricular structures at Evergreen are not responsive to the multiple identities of some Black males and Latinos. Unlike the extracurricular activities they participated in outside of school, school-sponsored clubs and organizations failed to provide them with anything of value. Similarly, Flores-Gonzalez (2002) found that the 22 low achievers in her study did not participate in school-sponsored activities because of their grades or because they were not interested in anything at the school. The significance is two-fold. First, the school does not value student participation in extracurricular activities outside of school. Second, non-participation creates unequal access to a network of resources that provides useful information about negotiating school. McNeal (1998) advises educators to attend to the patterns of youth's participation in extracurricular activities and the resulting benefits, such as successful negotiation of high-stakes tests and increased academic achievement, that youth can accrue based on their participation or lack thereof.

📖 **Reading in Action** 📖

1. In what ways have you seen teachers, counselors, and/or administrators support Black males' and Latinos' interests emerging from their cultural and academic identities?

2. Have you engaged Black males' and Latinos' perspectives and critique of schools' academic and extracurricular activities to change your practices? Why or why not?

3. How can you acknowledge and support the activities that students engage within their communities to facilitate their college readiness? When and how do you talk with students about what they are doing outside of school (e.g., writing assignments about youth's activities outside of school)?

IMPLICATIONS AND CONCLUSION

A school's responsiveness to Black males' and Latinos' academic and cultural intersecting identities impacts the type of policies, curricula, academic support, and extracurricular activities that are offered to support their college readiness. Educators who recognize the intersecting identities of Black males and Latinos have the potential to create and sustain culturally relevant policies and practices to enhance their educational achievement. We agree with many policymakers and researchers who critique the measure of academic achievement solely through standardized tests (Hurtado, 2003) and who push for creating school structures that support youth's connections and success in and out of school (Brown & Evans, 2002). However, as Hurtado (2003) notes, "If standardized testing is the barrier to getting students of color into college, then they [need to] push students to excel on these tests" (p. 219). Thus, in the spirit of "compliance and resistance simultaneously" (p. 219) to high school graduation exams and the necessity to create school structures that undergird Black males' and Latinos' success, we recommend the creation of culturally relevant policies and practices in two areas: rigorous academic preparation and extracurricular activities.

Academic Preparation

Organizational features within Evergreen High School, such as tracking structures, revealed the importance of teachers' curricular and pedagogical practices in shaping Black males' and Latinos' learning and state exam results. Geneva Gay (2010) argues that "scores on tests and grades students receive on classroom learning tasks to do not explain why they are not performing at acceptable levels. They are symptoms of, not causes of or remedies for, the problems" (p. 17). At least 70% of Evergreen's teachers have master's degrees and have been teaching for at least 5 years. Thus, the problem is not attributable to unqualified teachers or high rates of teacher turnover. Professional development around culturally relevant and meaningful curricular and teaching practices in a high-stakes testing environment is needed to enable teachers to assist Black male and Latino students in learning subject matter and passing Regents exams by building on their cultural backgrounds and assets. In addition, support within the school needs to be generated to enable educators to rethink negative consequences of school policies when students fail state exams. An enriched curriculum in their coursework that prepares students for the state exams also needs to emphasize accelerated learning rather than remediation. This would help to ensure that students who are placed in the general education courses—both Black students who have been in the United States for several generations and Latino students whose families are first-generation immigrants—have access to teachers as qualified and prepared as those of Black first- and 1.5-generation immigrant students in the honors courses. We also note that the three Black males in the study labeled "learning disabled" identified their resource teacher, whom they met with for one period each day, as providing the most academic support. This suggests the need for more collaboration between resource teachers and content area teachers to support the college readiness of students labeled "learning disabled." Finally, we argue that if teachers and counselors could incorporate more culturally responsive practices and policies that Black males have identified as important to their learning, the potential for their learning and achievement—and their successful negotiation of state exams—could be increased.

Extracurricular Activities

Opportunities for youth to participate in extracurricular activities are an untapped curricular innovation in the effort to create a culturally relevant, schoolwide, college-going culture. Researchers argue that inclusion in extracurricular activities facilitates inclusion and peer-related experiences, and a sense of belonging, which contribute to greater school connections and whether students attend postsecondary institutions (Hearn & Holdsworth, 2005). We further assert that access to cross-age peer and adult mentors builds teacher, student, and peer relationships that strengthen youth's cultural and academic identities while providing support for taking exams, sharing college information, and creating leadership opportunities for negotiating the complexities of college going. Specifically, schools can address the structural limitations of their extracurricular activities by building the capacity to offer a wide range of activities informed by youth's perspectives to ensure access and participation for more students. For example, promising strategies for increased participation in extracurricular activities could be accomplished through solicitation of youth's input about activities that are interesting and meaningful for them. The development of and greater participation in activities could be enhanced through surveys at the beginning of each year, as well as the creation of a schoolwide policy that increases youth's capacity to start new clubs during the year that meet their needs. Schools also can partner with communities to further support youth's academic achievement and social involvement by incorporating the recognition and awareness of their participation in community-sponsored activities. Opportunities to participate in extracurricular activities in school and out of school can promote increased student engagement in the school and facilitation of additional state exam requirements and college admissions information to enhance student achievement.

In sum, in the face of dismal educational achievement outcomes and reform efforts that seek to change this status, Black males and Latinos in our study have much to contribute to educators' understandings of what is supporting them (or not) as "successful negotiators" of college-going influences in and out of school. Schoolwide culturally relevant policies and practices based on their perspectives have the potential to better support Black males' and Latinos' intersecting cultural and academic identities and educational experiences, facilitate successful negotiations of state exams and high school graduation requirements, and increase access to a college of their choice.

TEACHER RESPONSE

A few days into my first year as a teacher, several 9th-graders peered into the open door of my classroom during lunch. "Miss, can we come in?" one of them asked. "Sure," I responded, wondering what they wanted to talk about. The students, three Latinos and a Black male, were enrolled in the English class I taught, and I assumed they had a question about something we were working on in class. But rather than approach me, Pedro, Gabriel, David, and Brian pushed a few desks together at the back of the classroom and pulled decks of Yu-Gi-Oh! trading cards from their backpacks.

It was a ritual that began that day and continued throughout that school year and into the next. Their play was punctuated by conversations between them and, increasingly, with me. Some days, they would share their observations about the school or ask questions about school structures and policies, such as why they had to take certain classes, or why some teachers seemed to give more homework than others. Other times, I'd walk over to check in on them, asking questions about the game they were playing, who was winning, and what strategies they most often used to try to win.

Over time, we developed relationships that blurred the boundaries between "official" class time and the time spent during those lunch periods. Formal discussions about class texts, writing assignments, and projects that started in class worked their way into informal conversations during lunch. We talked about the youth's interests outside of school and their plans for the future, providing insight that informed my teaching practices, classroom management style, and curricular decisions. While there were drawbacks to having these males spend their lunch periods inside my classroom (they were choosing not to join their peers in the cafeteria or to eat the lunch provided to them, while I spent one of my non-teaching periods supervising students), these limitations were far outweighed by the benefits generated in providing a space for students to engage in their interests outside of the official school curriculum. Just as the "non-successful negotiators" in the preceding chapter expressed disinterest in many of the extracurricular activities offered at Evergreen High School, neither Pedro, Gabriel, David, nor Brian was formally involved in traditional extracurricular activities in the school. Their self-organized Yu-Gi-Oh! club addressed their interests, supporting them in developing peer and teacher networks that facilitated their academic achievement. For example, none of the young men was initially a vocal student during class discussions and activities. Yet they laughed, debated, discussed, and analyzed one another's actions as they played with the trading cards, leading me to rethink my notions of these students' engagement with curricular materials. I began to organize Pedro, Gabriel, David, and Brian into a group during class, recognizing that they could support one another's academic achievement, even as they grew more comfortable asking me questions and contributing to class discussions. My experiences working with these youth encouraged me to seek out opportunities to support their interests and experiences outside of the official school curriculum and/or class meeting times (Marciano, 2004, 2005). For example, lunch time became a space for me to extend the relationships I developed in the classroom with additional students as they engaged the classroom space for a variety of purposes, such as working on group projects, reading independently, and practicing for upcoming performances.

Beyond supporting youth's out of school interests within school spaces, I also see the need to provide state exam preparation for all students in a way that is organized and purposeful, and that explicitly addresses how and why students will be tested, in order to support their academic success and college-going practices. We complete weekly essay assignments that use texts that are culturally relevant, such as *A Hope in the Unseen* (Suskind, 1999), to prepare students for completing the required essay portion of the exam; listen to radio podcasts from National Public Radio on topics of interest to youth, including movie reviews, to build the listening skills assessed on the exam; and engage in periods of sustained silent reading of texts chosen by youth, in an attempt to further develop the reading stamina needed to complete the 3-hour exam. Each unit ends with students' completion of a written reflection about what worked for them, and what didn't work, and suggestions for me to consider when teaching the unit again in the future.

As I prepare students to successfully complete the state exam for the content area I teach, I seek to develop youth's sociopolitical awareness. For example, I talk with students about where the exam fits into the high school graduation requirements, and how a score of 75% or higher will exempt them from taking remedial English classes should they choose to attend a City University of New York college or another university (City University of New York, 2011). Further, I access students' transcripts through an online system offered to teachers, parents, and students to review with youth how they are progressing toward graduation requirements, answering any questions they might have and directing them to appropriate resources as needed. Although the role of reviewing student transcripts is typically associated with guidance counselors, youth often interact with their teachers more frequently than with their counselors (Farmer-Hinton & McCullough, 2008). Teachers therefore may offer supplemental support and information to youth at times that may be more convenient for them, provided that teachers are aware of how to read student transcripts and are knowledgeable of the graduation requirements.

Questions and Actions for Individuals

1.   What extracurricular activities, if any, were you involved in throughout your schooling experiences? What facilitated or hindered your involvement? How did your involvement or non-involvement influence your engagement in academic behaviors and your relationships with your peers and other school personnel?
2.   Describe a recent conversation you've had with Black males and Latinos about going to college. How do you build relationships with Black male and Latino students in your school? How might your interests and hobbies assist you in developing relationships with youth that extend beyond the classroom?
3.   How does the course you teach, or other activities in which you engage with youth, fit into their preparation for high school graduation and access to college? What are the skills beyond those required for state exams that students need in order to be considered college-ready (e.g., the ability to collaborate, to engage technology, to conduct research and present findings, etc.)?

Questions and Actions for Small Groups
Within School Communities

1.   What culturally relevant policies and practices are in place for Black male and Latino students to share their perspectives of their educational experiences?
2.   Which youth, particularly among male students, are experiencing (or not) academic success, preparing to meet state graduation requirements, and/or engaging in extracurricular activities? How might more Black males and Latinos be supported in experiencing academic success, being prepared for state graduation requirements, and/or being involved in extracurricular activities?
3.   What institutional policies and practices are available to support Black males' and Latinos' academic achievement and engagement in extracurricular activities that build upon their cultural backgrounds, lived experiences, and interests?

Questions and Actions for Whole-School Communities

1.   What opportunities exist for teachers and school personnel, beyond counselors, to access and become knowledgeable about school-level data (e.g., students' transcripts, state exam scores, school accountability reports)? How might this data inform curricular and pedagogical practices? How might teachers and school personnel be

encouraged to talk with Black males and Latinos about their academic achievement and overall preparation for high school graduation and college readiness?

2. How do Black males and Latinos become active in extracurricular activities within the school? Which students are engaging (or not) in these activities? Why?

3. What opportunities exist for teachers and school personnel to talk with Black male and Latino students about their interests outside of school? What incentives, financial or otherwise, are available to teachers who choose to work with youth in extracurricular activities?

CHAPTER 5

Critical Literacies and Family Involvement

Envisioning Black Females' and Latinas' College and Career-Ready Futures

> You have [your] own idea of what you want to do with your college education, where you want it to take you. You have set a goal. . . . You want to become a veterinarian and you know that there are certain steps that you have to do to become a veterinarian. You know you have to go to college, from college to med school. And you're willing to take those steps or take whatever measures you need to fulfill those goals. . . . You're self-motivated. And that's the important thing that you need, that teenagers need, to become successful college graduates.
>
> —Tamia's mother, Black

> I had a teacher like that in junior high school. She was like you're not going to high school. So then, when 8th grade came along and the high school acceptance, she asked me why I didn't ask her for a recommendation. I said because you were not one of the few teachers that believed in me. . . . I am not a genius. I don't have good grades. . . . When I graduated, she looked at me, she goes surprisingly, you made it. So it's people like that . . . makes me want to prove them wrong, look I did it. Thank you for not encouraging me.
>
> —Crystal, Latina, student

As educators look around their classrooms, they are aware that there are more girls than boys in PreK–12 schools than at any time in history. Because close to 60% of U.S. college students are women, and women earn the majority of master's and doctorate degrees (U.S. Department of Education, 2012), many clearly see these facts as evidence of the gains and parity that girls and women have made across the spectrum of PreK–20 education. However, behind these statistics there are many educational disparities along racial and ethnic lines that need to be addressed if college access for Black females and Latinas is to increase. For example, nationally in the class of 2009, Asian and White females graduated from high school at 81.5% and 80.2%, respectively, while 64.1% of Latinas and 61.1% of Black females graduated that same year (Editorial Projects in Education Research Center, 2011; see Appendix A). Alongside these statistics is the call for educators to prepare young women for mastery of core subjects and for 21st-century skills such as becoming critical thinkers, problem solvers, communicators, media and digitally literate, and globally competent (Common Core State Standards, 2011; Goodwin, 2010; Mazerella, 2011).

For educators seeking to create conditions with more equitable educational and occupational experiences and outcomes for Black females and Latinas, culturally relevant educational practices are needed that incorporate their everyday experiences and build upon their literacy strengths (Knight, Dixon, Norton, & Bentley, 2006; Moll & Gonzalez, 2001). The Black female and Latina quoted above demonstrate how their critical literacies provide insight into who and what is facilitating or hindering their academic achievement and career futures. By critical literacies, we mean the ways in which these college-bound young women, along with their families and peers, enact practices of reading, writing, talking, analyzing, interpreting, critiquing, and communicating meaning about (in)equitable academic and college-going practices to (re)position themselves as college bound. The irony revealed in Crystal's excerpt highlights the difficulties of becoming a "successful" Latina high school graduate. With high school graduation rates for Latinas 20 points lower than for their Asian and White counterparts, it is an "incredible achievement despite low expectations" (Latina Feminist Group, 2001, p. 12) that Crystal was able to attend a competitive high school of her choice (Lopez, 2002). Crystal herself was aware that if she had been considered a "genius" it might have stimulated the teacher's belief in her as a Latina and supported her self-efficacy and motivation, academic and cultural identities, and career future (Gonzalez, Jovel, & Stoner, 2004; Weiler, 2000).

In this chapter we focus explicitly on the experiences and perspectives of the 12 Black females and Latinas in our study and how daily they enact critical literacies within and across their multiple worlds of families, peer culture, media, and schools to challenge stereotypical assumptions of their lives as college bound. We choose to focus this chapter specifically on the females' perspectives for two reasons. First, we see a need for differentiating culturally relevant educational practices to address the unique opportunities and challenges facing young women as they negotiate their gendered schooling experiences and seek access to college. Second, we seek to highlight the connections between critical literacy practices and college access as perceived by the female participants who, unlike their male counterparts, discussed these issues throughout their engagement in the study.

Throughout this chapter, we examine the academic preparation and literacy standards of college preparation and readiness that the females engage with their families at home and peers at school, and the implications for teachers, counselors, and administrators who support their college- and career-ready futures. We give examples of the culturally relevant collaborative critical conversations and interactions within youth's everyday lives that include analyzing, problem solving, and creating new knowledge (Common Core State Standards, 2011). We also demonstrate how these young women develop and critique understandings of educational and societal inequities for individual and collective understandings of college readiness and access. In the first example, we highlight their culturally relevant collaborative conversations and interactions that illustrate both the cultural knowledge and critical literacies that Black females and Latinas, their peers, and their families engage (Delgado Bernal, Aleman, & Carmona, 2008; Godinez, 2006; Tilman, 2006). In the second example, the Black females and Latinas discuss interviews they conducted with family members about their critical literacy practices and their cultural knowledge around the topic of college going. These critical literacy practices increase youth's college readiness and emphasize college-going students' cultural backgrounds, providing the "cultural scaffolding" deemed crucial for historically under-represented students (Corwin, Colyar, & Tierney, 2005). Taken together, these two examples illustrate how the culturally collaborative conversations within and among families, peers, and school staff contributed in different ways to four competency areas defined as beneficial to facilitating college readiness (Common Core State Standards, 2011; Corwin, Colyar, & Tierney, 2005): (1) academic preparation; (2) access to college-planning information and navigational strategies; (3) development of self-efficacy and college going, and (4) strategies of socialization and acculturation. While beneficial to both male and female students, we discuss how practices that consider these competency areas, alongside the gendered experiences of young women, may assist educators in further supporting the academic learning, cultural identities, and career futures of Black females and Latinas as college-bound youth.

YOUTH, MEDIA, AND COLLEGE READINESS

Youth today are increasingly engaged in varied forms of media, critical literacies, and technology (Kafia & Peppler, 2011; Vasudevan, 2010) that can anchor their learning in meaningful, culturally relevant collaborative conversations and interactions with peers and family members in and out of schools. The emphasis on girls and their futures is embedded within various

> ### 📖 Reading in Action 📖
>
> 1. Refer to the quotes at the beginning of this chapter and consider how these quotes reflect your ideas about the messages girls receive about their academic identities, learning, and their futures. Where do these messages come from (e.g., television, media, families)?
> 2. What kinds of messages do you send to Black and Latina students about their academic identities and futures? How do you think these messages differ if one is Asian, Black, Latina, Native American, and/or White? What are the consequences of these differing messages for facilitating or hindering Latina and Black students' college readiness?

media in television programs, including *Seventh Heaven, The Parkers*, and *Glee*; magazines directed at Black females and Latinas, such as *Latina, Vanidades*, and *Essence*; and YouTube videos. The Black females and Latinas in our study revealed their own self-efficacy with family members as they discussed and critiqued ideas about four television shows they watch. They actively sought out these shows to support their academic learning and preparation that they link to their college-going identities.

Notably, Tamia, one of the Black females in our study, remarked that she and her mother often watch TV together and during these shows her mother is quite explicit about the high academic expectations—not only for high school studies but also for college enrollment—she holds for her daughter. Tamia shared that the first conversation she had about college was with her mother. "We were watching some TV show and she said, 'You are going,' and I said, 'What' (laughter). You can go out of state, out of the country if you get a scholarship." At other times Tamia remarks that she mostly talks about education and college with her mother while watching television, specifically programs that share female characters' aspirations to attend college. "One time we watched *Seventh Heaven* and Mary decided that she wasn't going to college. She [my mother] turned around and was like, you're going (laughter). We were watching *The Parkers* and Kim said she wasn't going to college." Tamia told us her mother said, "You're going," and she responded, "I know."

Moreover, by focusing on college readiness and access in relation to the experiences of female characters on television, Tamia's culturally relevant conversations with her mother encompass the expectations of high-quality academic achievement for youth and the multiple levels of support and care for their well-being. Tamia specifically understands her mother's care through her statements such as, "I'm supporting you going to college by encouraging you, giving you moral support, as well as guides to supplement what you're getting in school so that you can make decent choices." School personnel may gain insight into the varied ways family members explicitly share with their daughters what their support or care looks like for their achieving their college-going goals (Knight, Oesterreich, & Newton, 2003; Sanders, 1998; Ware, 2006).

Other family members in the study explicitly share how they articulate their high academic expectations for their daughters. For example, Jackie's mother tells her, "I will support you emotionally, physically, financially, in every way that a parent possibly can. I encourage you to go and motivate you into getting your goals." Similarly, Marissa's cousin tells her that she "should work hard. He is always asking me about what college I want to go to. I asked him how does he like being in college? He told me . . . you can work hard and you can do it. He encouraged me." The "college talk" taking place among the young women and their family members offers understandings of how parents and family encourage youth's college aspirations through emotional, physical, and moral support. Some researchers, such as Tara Yosso (2005), would argue that this type of support, the family or community cultural wealth that families possess, is often hidden or invisible to school personnel. Families challenge traditional assumptions that they are not involved in fostering their children's college-going identities and how college decision making occurs.

📖 Reading in Action 📖

1. When you think of parent and family involvement in schools, what comes to mind? How are these ideas similar to or different from those being expressed by these Latinas and Black females and their families?

2. When you think of parent and family involvement in support of youth's college readiness, what images from television, movies, and/or video games come to mind? How might these images be connected to school curriculum, policies, and practices?

3. How do you and your colleagues value and build upon emotional, physical, and moral support for college readiness provided by families?

For many youth, varied forms of popular culture, such as movies, video games, technologies, comic books, and TV shows, offer additional culturally relevant funds of knowledge for them to draw upon in their decision-making efforts for their college and career readiness in their daily lives (Gee, 2007; Morrell, 2004). In the interaction between students' everyday experiences, school realities, and popular culture, youth construct their academic identities as they engage in the critical literacies of college readiness and preparation supported by the Common Core State Standards (2011). They also strengthen their critical literacy practices by developing and acting upon a sociopolitical awareness of educational and societal inequities impacting their own lives. Specifically, they engage in media literacies, which are defined as the "ability to access, analyze and engage in critical thinking about the array of messages people receive and send in order to make informed decisions about the everyday issues in their lives" (Hobbs, 2010, p. vii). As Montgomery, Gottlieb-Robles, and Larson (2004) note, this generation of young people is the "first to grow up in a world saturated with networks of information, digital devices and the promise of perpetual connectivity" (p. 1).

Although the female participants in our study are not alone in their engagement with media, the following focus group excerpt highlights the collaborative critical conversation, critical literacies, and interactions two girls, one Black and one Latina, Renee and Jessica, have about the role of television and how they perceive its value in the face of criticism from others. In the midst of negative criticism, they deliberately evaluate critiques of popular media, including television shows, and engage aspects of youth culture that others deem valueless. Jessica and Renee watch television shows that are helpful to them academically, culturally, and personally. Curiously enough, at one point, even when the university researcher tries to move away from the influence of TV on their college-going processes, the girls continue to discuss its value for them by naming and identifying their experiences with popular media (Mitchell & Reid-Walsh, 2007).

> *Researcher:* A lot of you talked about working toward going to college and wanting to do things like getting good grades, joining extracurricular activities, passing the Regents, going to tutoring, and I was wondering if there's anything specific that you think are a part of going to college or pursuing college?
>
> *Jessica* (10th-grade Latina): Watching TV is a good way.
>
> *Researcher:* How so?
>
> *Renee* (10th-grade Black female): I know people say worse things on TV, you only watch stupid things. . . . Like there's a cartoon called *Historia*, I used to watch it every day. I learned a lot of stuff, like the Civil War. You learn a lot of stuff on TV. My father goes, why are you always watching stupid stuff on TV? You know, I took this test, and the question says what is the Magna Carta and I remember saying the other night, there was this game called the Magna Carta and the object of the game is to take all the treasures and keep away the drought. . . . So, like, when I answered the question, it made it easier.

Researcher: Okay, so TV supports you in what you're doing. Is there anyone else, or who are some other groups of people that support you as you think of going on to college?

Renee: Actually, I think the History Channel. I think about it a little bit. It said something about Buddhism and Hinduism and all of that.

Jessica: On MTV, you learn a lot of words. . . . You're like, what does that word mean and stuff like that. That's how you learn words. TV is a good way to learn.

Historia, the History Channel, and MTV serve as examples of media that strengthen Black females' and Latinas' content literacy in social studies as well as providing information on important historical events. Renee specifically gained resources that prepared her to further problem solve the question in relation to the Magna Carta. The culturally relevant collaborative conversations also open up the opportunity for educators to understand how these shows support the Black females' and Latinas' capacity to develop their vocabularies and expand their understandings of language use in a variety of contexts. Further, in learning about the Magna Carta from television, Renee is analyzing "various accounts of a subject told in different mediums" (Common Core State Standards, 2011, p. 40).

In essence, these females enable educators to see how they interpret messages embedded within television shows differently based on the intersections of race/ethnicity, gender, class, and language ability. These women are engaging their critical literacies to integrate multiple sources of information presented in diverse formats and media (e.g., visually, quantitatively, orally) in order to make informed decisions and solve problems, evaluating the credibility and accuracy of each source and noting any discrepancies among data presented (Common Core State Standards, 2011). For instance, they critically analyze the media texts to evaluate the evidence against television shows and to "speak back" to a single interpretation of the media, specifically their TV viewing habits as "stupid" or as not an important influence by Renee's father and the researcher (Mallan & Pearce, 2003). Moreover, these Black females and Latinas provide insight into how they utilize their own agency to position themselves in more complex ways as college-bound youth who question and analyze varied college-going influences. Their culturally relevant critical literacies of college readiness, such as those of analysis, evaluation, and interpretation, position them as critics of their own worlds in their homes and schools and enable them to act in ways that support their academic and college-going aspirations and identities. Educators can build upon these females' culturally relevant critical literacies in their content subject areas, such as English, science, and social studies, and can further facilitate the young women's negotiations of college preparatory learning standards, such as reading standards that call upon students to analyze the explicit and implicit meanings of texts, including digital media (Common Core State Standards, 2011).

In imagining their futures, some of the Black females and Latinas engage in culturally relevant practices as they critically read the social worlds around them and envision their occupational place in society as well as a better life for themselves. For example, during an interview early in 9th grade, Abigail, a Black female, discusses how she sees herself as Max, a female Black lawyer who wore braids in affirmation of her cultural identity on the television show *Living Single. Living Single* followed the daily lives of four successful single Black women living in New York City. The life Max leads as a lawyer is highlighted in Abigail's reflections after her youth co-researcher interview with her family member. She stated:

> With me, the world teaches me that I have to go to college. Every day, I wake up and go outside I see things. I see people that are homeless and poor. I see people that are on drugs. I see people cleaning floors. When I see this I don't see me. The place I see me is graduating from college with high honors, going on to law school, wearing the business suits, winning just about every case I am given, making that money, living life to the fullest and more.

Instead of undermining her desire and agency in understanding how the world influences her future prospects, Abigail names and reads the messages of her immediate surroundings as those facilitating her sociopolitical awareness and her cultural identity as a college-bound Black female.

These young Black women and Latinas, Tamia, Jessica, Renee, and Abigail, reveal how detrimental it would be for educators and family members to position youth as lacking in critical thinking skills and agency in regard to the media. As Fisherkeller (1997) notes, the value of examining youth's watching of TV shows reveals the way youth employ "different kinds of cultural learning about self, social worlds and power" (p. 487). These young people illustrate how they make sense of their intersecting multiple worlds of home, the surrounding community, and TV to utilize their agency to construct their academic identities, affirm their cultural identities, and enhance their literacy learning.

YOUTH, INQUIRY PROJECTS, AND COLLEGE READINESS

The inclusion of youth co-researchers in inquiry projects, wherein youth work with teachers and/or researchers to gather data to be analyzed as part of a research study such as the one we conducted, provides academically

📖 **Reading in Action** 📖
1. What kinds of messages, such as those found in television, film, video games, and/or video-sharing websites, have you seen about Black females' and Latinas' learning, cultural identities, college aspirations, and goals? How do you reinforce or challenge representations of Black females and Latinas in popular media?   2. How do you think media images facilitate or hinder youth's critical literacy practices and college readiness? How can you build upon and support the critical literacies that Black females and Latinas engage in their interactions with popular culture in support of their college readiness?   3. How might you use various forms of media to strengthen Latinas' and Black females' academic identities, cultural identities, and college-going futures?

enriching, culturally supportive, and standards-based educational experiences for students, bringing together two influences that impact their college readiness and access: family members and the students themselves. First, youth co-researchers serve as excellent resources for schoolwide reform efforts that can reshape notions of family involvement situated in culturally relevant conversations about college readiness and access. Second, the inclusion of youth co-researchers promotes the development of their critical literacy practices as college-bound youth. For example, the Common Core State Standards (2011) call for students to "conduct short as well as more sustained research projects" (p. 46). The female youth co-researchers in our study worked collaboratively as they engaged four competency areas beneficial to facilitating college readiness: (1) academic preparation, (2) access to college information and navigation strategies, (3) further development of self-efficacy and college going, and (4) strategies of socialization and acculturation. In their work as youth co-researchers, in which they were asked to interview a family member about issues of college access, the young women learned to conduct research, design self-generated culturally relevant questions, and engage in reflective analysis of the process. The strategies and skills participants may gain through their participation align with those identified by the Common Core State Standards (2011) as necessary for youth's preparedness for college. For example, the Common Core Standards for English Language Arts call for students to "propel conversations by posing and responding to questions that probe reasoning and evidence; ensure a hearing for a full range of positions on a topic or issue;

clarify, verify, or challenge ideas and conclusions; and promote divergent and creative perspectives" (Common Core State Standards, 2011, p. 50). Further, Ladson-Billings (2002) argues that high-quality academic achievement means that students are capable of doing something with knowledge other than repeating and reproducing it, while strengthening their cultural identities and developing a sociopolitical consciousness. The youth co-researchers created new knowledge, explanations, and understandings of the college-going process for themselves and one another through an authentic and highly engaging learning opportunity, which further facilitated their motivation and desires to be "college ready."

For their interviews with family members, the youth co-researchers generated 36 new questions. Their questions fell into the following categories: high school to college connections, family experiences in college, the role of race/ethnicity in their lives, financial aid, and future-oriented questions. Examples of these self-generated questions are outlined in Table 5.1.

Table 5.1. Youth Co-Researcher Inquiry Project with Family Members

High School to College Connections	Family Experiences in College	The Role of Race/ Ethnicity in Their Lives	Financial Aid	Future-Oriented Questions
Is college any different from high school?	How do you think going to college the first time impacted your going the second time?	What does being Latino/Hispanic mean to you?	Before going to college, were you on any teams that would help you get a scholarship?	Do you want me to go away to college or stay here?
What is it like not completing your high school education?	Who are the people you talked to about college when you were younger?	What are your disadvantages and advantages of being a minority?	Why didn't you try to get a scholarship?	Do you think that people who don't go to college can make it in life?
In high school were you on any teams or anything?	As a child was college discussed much?	When you hear about all the stereotypes about minorities, what do you think?	What if we don't have enough money to support me going to college?	What do you want me to learn in college?

The Black females and Latinas set priorities through their questions to gather knowledge about the college-going process of which they were not aware and about which they felt their parents and family members had specific cultural knowledge, thereby highlighting cultural assets family members possessed (Yosso, 2005). What links many of these questions is an understanding of what college will mean for them and their families. College going is not a singular experience situated solely with the females, but rather a collective endeavor affecting entire families. Their questions also reveal how much the youth co-researchers wanted to understand from their family members what experiences were like in their homes, high schools, colleges, and lives as influenced by race and ethnicity. Similar to Yonezawa and Jones's (2009) study, youth's family members highlighted "structural and cultural impediments to learning and achievement" (p. 208) the family members themselves experienced. For example, the females expressed concern about the advantages or disadvantages they will have in life depending on whether they attend college. Questions dealing with race and ethnicity speak to the young women's cultural identities and the critical awareness needed to navigate schooling environments as a racial or ethnic minority. These questions further speak to how a good "fit" between colleges and students' academic and cultural identities must be considered when choosing a college to attend. Family members' responses to the questions illustrate how they could facilitate the college readiness of the Black females and Latinas. The females' participation as youth co-researchers in this inquiry project engaged culturally relevant practices, built upon their perspectives and involvement in their own learning inclusive of their family members, and supported their college readiness and college-going futures.

IMPLICATIONS AND CONCLUSION

Drawing attention to the racial/gender gap of Black females' and Latinas' graduation from high school and enrollment in college opens up opportunities to consider how best to support their college readiness and access. The 12 Black and Latina youth in our study negotiate multiple influences, such as popular media, family and peer involvement, and culturally relevant curricular projects, that facilitate their academic achievement, educational opportunities, and college access. Through a focus on popular media and youth co-researcher processes, these young women persist in affirming their college-going identities. In doing so, they expand, in two distinct ways, the arc of possibilities for teachers, counselors, and administrators to understand and support their student learning, build on their critical literacies, and facilitate their sociopolitical awareness of how race and gender impact their college access. First, culturally relevant curricular and pedagogical

---

📖 Reading in Action 📖

1. What opportunities do you provide for Black females and Latinas to develop, critique, and present research on topics connected to their cultural identities and experiences? How might you create opportunities inclusive of youth's interests, self-generated questions, and critique of racial and/or gender inequities?

2. How might you provide opportunities for females to engage research that connects their experiences in and out of the classroom, especially in regard to media and popular culture, to foster culturally relevant practices building on their critical literacies and cultural specific knowledge?

3. What types of collaborative, inquiry-based research projects do you think support greater student voice and engagement in schools, and build upon the cultural resources and critical literacies of students?

---

practices can support the four identified dimensions of college readiness and Common Core State Standards (2011) toward preparing young females as college bound. For example, their self-reliance, academic learning, and cultural identities were supported through their critical literacy practices. Second, these Black females and Latinas open up new understandings of parent/family involvement in the college-readiness and access process. For instance, the inclusion of popular media and the youth co-researcher process provided insight into females' engagement as learners while incorporating family members' perspectives, which are essential influences in youth's college-going processes. Females relied on and utilized their cultural wealth, as individuals and collectively with their families, in support of college preparation and readiness. As young women who engage in critical literacy practices through interactions with media and youth co-researcher processes, they demonstrate that they are not only objects of data collection measuring academic achievement, but are powerful partners with teachers, administrators, and counselors in creating culturally relevant, schoolwide, college-going curricular and pedagogical practices.

TEACHER RESPONSE

I first began asking students to write a college essay as part of the 11th-grade English class I taught a few years ago. The assignment is designed to expose students to the college application questions featured on the Common

Application (2012), used by more than 400 colleges and universities to determine admission, while teaching to the Common Core State Standards (2011), which call for students to be able to produce writing that is "clear and coherent" and "in which the development, organization, and style are appropriate to task, purpose, and audience" (p. 41). While students typically approach the assignment with an excitement for exploring what they want to write about in their college essays, few choose to write about an issue of concern and its importance to them, even though they are directly impacted by issues such as social inequality, pollution, and health concerns. Eager to facilitate students' development of college essay responses to a number of prompts so they might choose their best work to send off with their college applications, I shared with them examples of essays featured in college preparation texts. Even after reading sample essays, students struggled with how to identify issues that mattered to them and were personal enough to be the focus of a college essay. That's when I began to expand my considerations of what constituted a classroom "text."

At a time when youth are gaining exposure to an expanding array of media, including television programs, movies, short films, and podcasts, opportunities exist to incorporate such media into curriculum, further developing the critical literacy practices youth need to be "college-ready." I needed to move past my perceptions of teaching and learning that privileged traditional notions of reading and writing to consider the multimodal texts many students engage. As Jewitt (2005) argues, I saw the need for my practices "to look beyond the linguistic" (p. 315). The move didn't come easily. I worried that showing videos in class would lead my colleagues to perceive me as an ineffective teacher, particularly if students were staring passively at the television. My engagement in a course focused on culture, media, and education as part of my doctoral studies, however, facilitated my ability to more clearly see ways to incorporate culturally relevant media into curriculum. I expanded the college essay unit, including clips from the television series *Brave New Voices* (Simmons, 2009), which follows youth who participate in a national poetry slam competition. After students watched performances in which the Black and Latina/o youth featured in the series discussed issues of social importance, their engagement with self-generated discussion questions proved that my fears that they would be passive viewers were unwarranted. Further, their active engagement led many students to write compelling college essays about issues that mattered to them.

Beyond supporting students' writing of the college essay, incorporating culturally relevant media into classroom practices may further develop youth's involvement in research projects. Resources such as the Media That Matters (2012) website feature short films about a variety of topics of social importance for writing college essays and serving as mentor texts for youth looking to research and create their own multimodal texts. For example, students I work with recently created PowerPoint presentations about issues such as same-sex marriage, teenage pregnancy, and bullying, after gathering evidence from short films they viewed on the Media That Matters website, making "strategic use of digital media in presentations . . . " (Common Core State Standards, 2011, p. 50).

As technological advances make media more accessible both to teachers and to youth, opportunities exist to build upon youth's cultural knowledge through the incorporation of such media into classroom practices, extending the school curriculum to incorporate cultural perspectives into content and materials of interest to female students. As Ladson-Billings (1994b) argues, when teachers search for additional materials and resources that reflect a range of cultural perspectives, "students learn more content and develop a real ability to ask and answer critical questions" (p. 24). So even though school Internet filters prevent me from sharing YouTube videos with my students, the filters do not block the websites of television networks that post episodes of programs online, or the Netflix website. Netflix, for example, features a variety of movies, documentaries, and television programs available for streaming online for a monthly fee, serving as another resource for supplementing traditional school curriculum resources with those that may enhance the academic identities and affirm the cultural identities of Black females and Latinas. These resources create opportunities for youth to engage in social critique through the curriculum, including youth inquiry projects that bring the critical literacy skills they demonstrate outside of school into school-sanctioned activities and assignments.

Questions and Actions for Individuals

1.   Describe the types of media (television, film, music, etc.) you typically engage. Would you consider yourself to be critical of this media (e.g., discussing it with family members or peers, questioning the content, seeking out further information from a different perspective about the content)? What leads you to be critical of this media? What role does race, ethnicity, age, and/or gender play in your critique?
2.   Describe a recent conversation you've had with Black females and Latinas about going to college. In what ways did this conversation support students' critical literacies and cultural identities?
3.   What media do the youth you work with typically engage? How do you know? What opportunities exist to talk with youth about the television programs, movies, music, and/or video games they interact with? How might you expand the materials and curriculum you engage with youth to be more inclusive of a variety of cultural

perspectives? What might assist you in incorporating a variety of media reflective of youth's cultural backgrounds into your interactions with youth?

Questions and Actions for Small Groups Within School Communities

1. What assumptions do you hold about the incorporation of media (e.g., television, movies, music, video games, etc.) into school curricular practices? How might you consider those assumptions? How might those assumptions facilitate and/or hinder youth's engagement in the curriculum?

2. Discuss the opportunities to connect your curriculum and pedagogy to media reflecting students' cultural backgrounds, experiences, and interests. If no such opportunities exist, how might you be supported to develop culturally relevant media curriculum?

3. How might your curriculum support youth in developing youth co-researcher projects? How might youth be supported in creating and sharing media that reflects their cultural backgrounds, including race, ethnicity, gender, age, and/or experiences?

Questions and Actions for Whole-School Communities

1. Discuss the schoolwide policies and structures that influence whether and how media and youth co-researcher inquiry are incorporated into curriculum and pedagogy. What resources (e.g., televisions, computers, Internet access, video cameras, cell phones, etc.) are available to facilitate youth's engagement with media (e.g., television, movies, music, video games, etc.) and research in school settings?

2. What opportunities exist for students to make connections between the media they engage with outside of school and their in-school practices? For example, what clips from different media that students engage with can you incorporate into the curriculum? How do those media represent youth and how might they support (or not) youth's academic identities and career futures?

3. How might youth co-researcher projects provide insight into youth's perspectives of school policies and practices? What connections beyond those discussed in this chapter can you make between youth co-researcher inquiry projects and the Common Core State Standards?

CHAPTER 6

Culturally Relevant Peer Groups, Friendships, and College Support

When I choose my friends, I choose someone that's like, more like me. They just want to go to school, do what they have to do, and that's it. They don't want to deal with all those other things at night, those negative things, they just want to deal with the positive, and that's it.

—Tamia, Black, female

You can use me as an example as to why you should go to school, because I may have an okay job, I may have a nice car, but I'm breaking my back to do it. Now wouldn't you rather make the same money sitting at a desk, you know, and just using your mind instead of your muscles and breaking your back all day long? I would prefer a desk job, you know?

—Angel, Latino

Some of my friends, some of my people from when I was like 9 years old . . . he was like he ain't go to college, 'cause he can't, 'cause there was certain things he did when he was my age. And I was talking to him. I don't wanna end up like that. So, it took somebody that's my age to let me see what ya'll been tryin' to tell me all this time.

—Abraham, Black, male

In the quotations above, Tamia, Angel, and Abraham highlight the multiple ways youth's peers provide encouragement, insight, and motivation as they engage in the college-going processes of preparing for, applying to, and enrolling in college. Not only are youth seeking out relationships with peers who share similar academic and life goals, as Tamia does, but as Angel and Abraham demonstrate, youth are teaching from their own experiences and learning from the experiences of their peers as they negotiate the mixed messages of college going described in Chapter 2. These youth's comments are particularly insightful as they interrupt traditional conceptions of youth peer groups, which frequently position teenagers as belonging to a subculture that operates in opposition to the aims of parents and teachers (Ryan, 2001). For example, Stanton-Salazar and Spina (2005) argue that ". . . many adults regard peer groups as the instigators of all the problems we commonly associate with adolescence" (p. 381). These perceptions may be informed by popular media portrayals of youth peer groups that often focus on negative aspects of peer pressure, including drug and alcohol abuse, and youth's engagement in violent behavior (Trier, 2005). Yet even though youth peer groups are depicted negatively in popular culture, and traditional notions of peer influence may be deficit-oriented, we argue that the relationships youth share with their peers extend traditional notions of culturally relevant pedagogy to provide unique sites of possibility for understanding how caring, connected relationships among peers increase college access for Black and Latina/o youth.

In this chapter, we identify the culturally relevant peer interactions taking place among youth in and outside of schools to support their college-going identities. As we explore the multiple and shifting roles peers play in influencing the college-going practices of youth, we draw upon Lewis-Charp, Yu, and Friedlaender's (2004) definition of peers as "friends, classmates, those who share extracurricular activities, and schoolmates" (p. 110). We define culturally relevant peer interactions as the ways youth provide academic and emotional support and gain encouragement from their peers in culturally relevant ways while engaging in college-going processes. For example, youth draw upon their shared cultural backgrounds and experiences as students attending an urban public high school as they exchange information about the financial costs of attending college, discuss and debate high school graduation requirements, and share high expectations for one another's futures. In highlighting these culturally relevant peer interactions, we build upon more recent educational research literature that emphasizes the positive roles peers may play in one another's lives (Gibson, Gándara, & Koyama, 2004). For example, as children become teenagers, the opinions of parents often become valued less as youth turn instead to their peers for validation and acceptance (Center for Higher Education Policy Analysis, n.d.). This is particularly true in the context of education, where youth are making decisions about how and why to engage in schooling based on their relationships with one another.

Throughout this chapter we focus on the experiences of six youth who interact with their peers in support of their college readiness and access: Gary and Abraham (classmates and friends); Crystal, Abraham, and Jessica (older peers within school); Crystal and Abraham (older peers in college); and Raquel and Angel (friends outside of school).

📖 Reading in Action 📖

1. Refer to the quotes at the beginning of this chapter and reflect on how these quotes reflect your ideas about how youth are influenced by their peers.
2. How do you think you were influenced by your peers in high school?
3. Describe how and why you think youth interact with their peers. How might the assumptions you make about these interactions influence your work with youth?

As we examine the role of peers in Black and Latina/o youth's college-going processes, we consider how culturally relevant peer interactions illuminate teaching and learning that emerge from peers' conceptions of self and others, how social relationships among them are engaged, and varied understandings of knowledge. These understandings and conceptions of teaching and learning support peers' academic achievement, cultural competence, and sociopolitical awareness. As a result, we make explicit reference to how youth participants in our study discussed and acted upon the information, insights, experience, and expertise they gained from their peers in those areas. In addition, we highlight and suggest opportunities for teachers, counselors, and administrators to build upon youth's existing peer relationships to further support their engagement in college-going processes as collaborators in the learning process.

PEER FOCUS #1:
GARY AND ABRAHAM (CLASSMATES AND FRIENDS)

In considering how and why peers influence youth's engagement in college-going processes, we first consider how friends enrolled in the same grade level at Evergreen High School informed each other's considerations of college going. The relationship between Gary and Abraham provides one example of how friends enrolled in the same grade at the same school may provide insight into high school graduation requirements, college enrollment requirements, and the process of applying for financial aid. For example, youth's (un)familiarity with the differences between high school graduation and college admissions requirements provided opportunities for exchanges such as the one below. The participants' conversation demonstrates aspects of culturally relevant peer interactions by supporting academic achievement, focusing on the importance of taking and passing a number of state-mandated exams, also known as the Regents, in order to graduate from high school with an advanced diploma.

> *Abraham*: I wasn't really worrying about failing or passing, because they told me, you only need one Regents. Nobody cares about Regents diploma, not me.
> *Michelle* (Interviewer): You don't care about Regents diploma? Why not?
> *Abraham*: I care about SAT, the SAT, the S-A-T, and all that.
> *Gary*: You've got to graduate, though.
> *Abraham*: You just need one to graduate. Wait a minute.
> *Gary*: You need science, global, history, you've got to take two to have the Regents.
> *Abraham*: No, I'm talking about for science—I'm talking about for science Regents.
> *Gary*: What?
> *Abraham*: So if I fail science Regents, I could take biology Regents or chemistry Regents.
> *Gary*: You don't want either one.
> *Abraham*: Why not?
> *Gary*: Because you just take it like earth science.
> *Abraham*: You mean drop science?
> *Gary*: Biology is. . . . And chemistry is real hard, I heard.
> *Abraham*: You're not going to take chemistry?
> *Gary*: Next year. Now, I've got to take it.
> *Abraham*: And you've got to take it—exactly. But even if you fail, you already got by on your Regents.

While one might draw upon traditional conceptions of schooling and expect that Abraham should turn to his guidance counselor to learn about the number of state-mandated Regents exams he must pass in order to graduate from Evergreen High School, his conversation with his friend Gary serves as an example of how and why youth are turning to their peers to gain information about engaging in college-going processes, especially the role of testing in this process and the rigor of their academic course load. Abraham's relationship with Gary provides ample opportunities for the two friends to exchange information about college-going processes. This is especially important considering the comparatively limited opportunities the youth had to access their guidance counselors. While Gary's source of information about the differences between the courses students must take and the exams they must pass is unclear, Abraham asks him questions— "What?" "Why not?" "You're not going to take chemistry?"—signaling his desire to consider Gary's perspective and to gain insight from his experience. Later in the conversation, Abraham and Gary extend their discussion of high school graduation requirements to consider the colleges they may be interested in applying to and the costs associated with attending them.

> *Abraham*: I mean, New York is so expensive, man, you want to be paying for college.
>
> *Gary*: Because my school is just like, depends on the school, because there'll be schools like—tuition.
>
> *Michelle*: It depends on the school.
>
> *Gary*: The school, yeah. Like, if you want to go to Columbia, you're going to have to pay, Fordham, you're going to have to pay. And some schools you don't have to pay as much.
>
> *Abraham*: I want to go to a school that I don't have to pay as much.
>
> *Gary*: But you've got financial aid, though, it depends on how much your family makes, your income, you get financial aid, and your parents pay for the rest.

Again, Gary shares information about engaging in college-going processes, in this case, paying for college, with Abraham. Although the information Gary shares is limited in its specificity—"you've got financial aid . . . you get financial aid"—he demonstrates his willingness to share information with his friend, creating an opening for future discussions between teachers, counselors, and youth about applying for financial aid or paying for college. Unlike peer-mentoring programs that train youth as counselors whose responsibility it is to share information about college with students who approach them for assistance, the support Gary and Abraham provide to each other in their conversations about academic requirements and paying for college arises out of their friendship. Such opportunities for conversation may be more frequent, and build upon previously established and culturally relevant understandings about one another's experiences and goals. Schools may provide support for youth to informally share information about college going with their friends by encouraging students to talk with one another about what they know about preparing for and applying to college. For example, teachers may begin conversations with youth about engaging in college-going processes during classroom interactions, suggesting that students continue to share their ideas and questions with one another as they move through the hallways or eat lunch together. Teachers, guidance counselors, and administrators also may encourage youth to attend college tours with their peers, sharing information via college websites about how to schedule campus visits during school breaks and about applying for financial aid. Further, guest speakers who have attended college, including school alumni, may visit with students during their lunch periods or after school to share their experiences and to answer questions.

📖 Reading in Action 📖

1. How might you facilitate culturally relevant peer interactions that support youth's college-going identities?
2. In what ways might you provide opportunities for friends enrolled in the same grade to gain opportunities within school contexts, such as during college visits and college fairs, to collaborate and share information about preparing for, applying to, and attending college?
3. What, if any, structures have you seen schools create to provide peers with opportunities to share information about the financial aid process in connection to attending a range of postsecondary institutions?

PEER FOCUS #2: CRYSTAL, ABRAHAM, AND JESSICA (LEARNING FROM OLDER PEERS IN SCHOOL)

In addition to providing and gaining support related to college going in their interactions with peers enrolled in the same grade at Evergreen High School, youth participants also described their interactions with youth who were in higher grades as sources of information and knowledge about engaging in college-going processes. These youth are capable of engaging in culturally relevant peer interactions, particularly because they have engaged in college-going processes themselves. Rather than having to rely solely on teachers, guidance counselors, and administrators for firsthand knowledge about what it means to prepare for, apply to, and enroll in college, youth are able to gather such information and knowledge from peers familiar with the school culture in which youth currently engage. For example, in a focus group interview, Crystal, Abraham, and Jessica discussed how Crystal gained information and knowledge about completing the college application process from a 12th-grade student she knew.

> Like this one girl, she didn't think she was going to make it into her college, but you know, she struggled, she got her recommendations, she got in. She tells you, it could get you quite depressed to look at the top college, the one you want the most, [and it] doesn't pick you.

The culturally relevant peer interactions provide opportunities to build upon a shared secondary schooling experience to address the emotional and logistical challenges associated with applying to college. The memory of what the 12th-grade student said influences Crystal's understandings of what it takes to apply to college and the emotional response that she may have ("it could get you quite depressed" to apply to colleges that don't offer admission) if her top choice doesn't select her. Further, in recalling that this older peer within her school "didn't think she was going to make it into her college," and that she "struggled" before gaining college admission, Crystal demonstrates sociopolitical awareness in understanding the reality of what applying to college may really be like. This awareness is further magnified when considering that not only are Black and Latina/o youth in New York City graduating from high school at rates below the national average (Editorial Projects in Education Research Center, 2011), but even fewer Black and Latina/o youth are attending college (U.S. Department of Education, 2012). Crystal's older peer expresses the self-doubt and uncertainty that comes with applying to college, particularly for youth attending urban public schools who are typically less prepared to engage in a rigorous academic curriculum in college than students attending more affluent suburban schools (McDonough, 1997).

In seeking out information from an older peer who applied to college, Crystal demonstrates her desire to learn about overcoming the challenges one might experience in completing the process from the standpoint of someone who has a shared secondary schooling experience. She continues by saying, "I got a lot of different impacts from a lot of different seniors," signaling a repeated attempt to access information about engaging in college-going processes from several peers who had personal experience in doing so. Possibilities exist for school personnel to build upon culturally relevant peer interactions by providing opportunities for cross-age peer mentoring that facilitates communication among students across grade levels. This can happen either through formal schoolwide structures such as curricular projects that team students from differing grades together and school-site college fairs for 9th- through 12th-graders, or through more informal avenues, such as arranging for groups of students from different grades to attend field trips together during which opportunities for youth to interact are likely to arise.

PEER FOCUS #3:
CRYSTAL AND ABRAHAM
(LEARNING FROM OLDER PEERS ATTENDING COLLEGE)

For youth who are the first in their families to prepare for and apply to college, opportunities to learn from peers who currently are attending college provide access to information about logistical aspects of the experience that otherwise might not be available to them (Knight, Oesterreich, & Newton, 2003). These opportunities are particularly urgent for low-income youth, including those who have received free and reduced meals throughout their public schooling experiences, as they may have questions about the financial aspects of attending college. The conversation below, from a focus group interview, provides one example.

> *Abraham*: I think about the food situation. Like if I go far away, like spending money on food [is] expensive. So I heard some of them have like a lunch thing you can go in . . . and that you gotta pay a certain amount of money. I'd rather have that than to have to go outside and pay whatever the food is out there.
>
> *Crystal*: I know somebody that, um, they went to this school upstate, and they have this thing inside the school, this all you could eat thing, but then they give you points. And let's say like you eat a lot . . . but you get 24 points a week, and you go to the all you can eat place and that costs like two points, right. Let's say you don't want that anymore . . . so maybe you'll order whatever you want from McDonald's and that'll cost you like four points. And if you spend all your points then you just gotta be hungry for the rest of the week.

In beginning the discussion by referring to "the food situation," Abraham calls attention to the idea that there could, in fact, be a "situation" related to getting food while attending college. While upper and middle class college applicants may be less likely to worry about whether they will be able to obtain food on a daily basis, or go hungry, Abraham and Crystal demonstrate a shared interest in understanding the logistics associated with eating meals on a college campus. Unlike youth whose parents have attended college and who are more likely to be able to share their own experiences about how the dining hall system may operate, Abraham and Crystal instead turn to peers who are attending college in search of culturally relevant, college-going information.

📖 **Reading in Action** 📖
1.   How have you seen youth's relationships with peers already attending college influence their decisions to prepare for, apply to, and enroll in college?
2.   How can you facilitate interactions between high school students and those already in college? How might such interactions address issues of educational equity?

PEER FOCUS #4: RAQUEL AND ANGEL
(LEARNING FROM FRIENDS OUTSIDE OF SCHOOL)

The final peer relationship we examine is that of Raquel and Angel. The two are neither classmates nor schoolmates, but rather share a friendship outside of the context of school, a relationship that, in some cases, also may be viewed as extended family (Knight, Dixon, Norton, & Bentley, 2006). Even so, Raquel identified Angel as someone who supports her academic aspirations of attending college, choosing to interview him as part of the youth co-researcher aspect of the research study. Raquel's decision to interview Angel stands out from the decisions made by the other participants to interview a family member who supports their engagement in college-going processes. In a written journal response, Raquel explains what led her to make that decision: "The reason I have chosen to interview Will as opposed to my mother or any other family member is because I feel that he is the only person who would really be proud of me." Raquel's reasoning echoes the findings of research conducted by Stanton-Salazar and Spina (2005) that found the peer network was seen by adolescents as "being more supportive than any other" (p. 383), including youth's family members. By identifying Angel as "the only person who would really be proud of me," Raquel highlights the powerful role peers can play in providing positive support in achieving one another's goals. Raquel furthers this idea in a subsequent journal entry when she writes about Angel's answer to her interview question about how he supports her in preparing for college:

> He said that he'd support me in every way (How sweet! (lol)) he also went on to say that even though it will be rough, he knows that I'll make it. NOW THAT'S SUPPORT! So yea, that's really important, emotionally, one needs all the support one can get (ESPECIALLY THIS ONE . . . me). Again, I really like his answer to this one. Notice not one mention of money. Not one doubt of my success. And it was all said with the utmost sincerity!

In recalling Angel's response, Raquel highlights his engagement of culturally relevant peer interactions in his vocalization of high expectations for her academic success. By stating that "he knows that I'll make it," Angel explicitly states his expectation that Raquel will be successful in college. Yet what is perhaps even more notable than Angel's words of support is Raquel's reaction to it. Her excitement over his response is visible in her use of capital letters to spell out her interpretation of his response: "NOW THAT'S SUPPORT!" The idea of support is visible in another section of a journal entry written by Raquel:

The reason why Angel is the one who influences me to go to college
is because I know that in the end he'll be proud of me because of my
achievement. . . . Also because in the years that I've known him, he has
done a lot for me, he has helped me a great deal and I don't want it all
to have been in vain. Besides, there is nothing that I find more delight in
than to see Angel happy and I walk up in my cap and gown and receive
my diploma.

The trust developed between Raquel and Angel seems to play a role
in her desire to achieve her goal of attending college, particularly if breaking her promise and not attending college could be a disappointment to
him. The role of trust, particularly "the expectation that friends will not
reveal confidences [and] will not break promises," plays an important role
in youth's peer relationships (Stanton-Salazar & Spina, 2005, p. 386).

Although Raquel and Angel are peers who share a friendship outside
of the context of a shared schooling experience, opportunities exist within
schools to extend Raquel's friendship with Angel to further support her
engagement in college-going processes, particularly as related to her success
once enrolled in college. For example, in interviewing Angel, Raquel asks
him, "In what ways do you support me going to college?" Angel expresses
an interest in doing whatever he can to assist her. For example, he shares:

I support your learning in every which way possible to do so, because
I know once you're in there, it'll be rough, but I know you'll make it.
. . . If you needed a study partner, I'm here for you. Anything, anything,
anything that you would need. I mean, I've never experienced college
personally, so I wouldn't know exactly what. But you know, whichever
you would need me to be there for you, I would be.

Angel's eagerness to support Raquel's engagement in college-going processes "in every way" is complicated by his lack of understanding what
specifically he can do to support her success. Rather than describe explicit
strategies for supporting Raquel, Angel broadly speaks of acting as a "study
partner." However, his interactions with Raquel are culturally relevant as
they build upon her lived experiences and promote high expectations for
her achievement, demonstrated by his expectation that she will "make it."
Angel further encourages Raquel's development of sociopolitical awareness
by highlighting the broader issues of inequity that may complicate her experiences attending college. For example, Angel says, ". . . once you're in
there, I know it'll be rough . . ." Although he does not state exactly how he
knows "it'll be rough," Angel points out to Raquel that attending college
is not likely to be the smooth experience depicted in most popular culture
conceptions of college experiences. Further, by mentioning that he has not

attended college himself, Angel complicates notions of college access, particularly when his comments are considered alongside his words featured at the beginning of this chapter: "Now wouldn't you rather make the same money sitting at a desk, you know, and just using your mind instead of your muscles and breaking your back all day long?" Angel offers a critical critique of his positioning in society and implies that by obtaining a college degree, Raquel won't have to engage in physically taxing labor in the way that he does. As a result, he influences her considerations of how obtaining a college degree could affect the type and quality of future work in which she engages.

📖 Reading in Action 📖

1.   Who do you see as culturally relevant role models for Black and Latina/o youth? How do the different types of peer relationships described in this chapter further support your understandings of who can be a role model in the college-going process?
2.   What possibilities exist in your work with youth for making connections between their engagement in college-going processes and their relationships with friends outside of school contexts?
3.   How do you think youth's friends in out of school contexts can facilitate their understandings of the advantages of having a college degree versus a high school diploma?

IMPLICATIONS AND CONCLUSIONS

The four kinds of peer relationships described above, peers as friends and classmates, older peers within school, older peers in college, and friends outside of school, highlight culturally relevant ways youth support and encourage one another in preparing for, applying to, and enrolling in college. Youth clearly are providing culturally relevant information about engaging in these college-going processes, and offer insight for one another that resonates because it engages their frames of references and facilitates learning that supports healthy academic and cultural identities that are jointly constructed with their peers. Yet even as youth engage in their support of peers, school structures and practices often limit opportunities for youth to collaborate with one another in meaningful ways. For example, curriculum and pedagogy that limit opportunities for youth to work collaboratively with one another often fail to acknowledge and build upon the powerful role youth play in one another's emotional, social, and academic development.

By seeking out support from their peers in engaging in college-going processes, youth emphasize the value they place on learning from their peers, who often are perceived as being better able to relate to the experiences of the youth themselves. This finding is especially notable when considering the ethnic/social class/educational background(s) of youth's teachers and guidance counselors in relation to the youth themselves. For example, as previously noted, many urban teachers come from White middle class backgrounds, while their students are often Black and Latina/o and from working class backgrounds. Therefore, it is necessary to provide opportunities for working class youth to talk with their peers about issues of importance to them, such as how they will get food, which may not be issues many of their teachers, particularly those from upper and middle class backgrounds, have experience with.

TEACHER RESPONSE

On my first day as a teacher, I stood at the classroom doorway with a stack of index cards in my hand, carefully labeled with a letter/number combination (i.e., A1, B1, C1, etc.) that corresponded to a desk inside the classroom. I planned to hand a card to each of the 9th-graders in the English class I taught as they entered the classroom, directing them to an "assigned" seat. As I awaited the students' arrival, I purposefully mixed up the cards so students who walked in together would not sit next to each other. I settled on this system after weeks of worrying about how I was going to prevent students from sitting with their friends inside the classroom. My biggest concern about my teaching was whether I would be able to "control" the class. I previously had attended pre-service teacher workshops focused on classroom management, read books and articles on the subject, and talked with family members and friends who were teachers about the strategies they used to keep students on task. Although the techniques they described differed, one piece of advice remained consistent across a variety of school contexts: Don't let students sit with their friends.

The advice didn't really surprise me, which is perhaps why I so eagerly adopted the assigned seating system described above. Teenage peer groups often are considered by adults to be sources of negative influences, particularly as related to student academic performance. As I began to spend time with youth I taught, however, I began to pay closer attention to how they supported one another academically, challenging my own assumptions that youth were distracting influences for one another. I noticed that students who appeared to be off task during independent work periods actually were providing clarification to peers about the task in which they were supposed to engage. At the back of the classroom, one student copied from another's notes because she found it easier than straining to read from the chalkboard at the front of the room. After sharing their written work in pairs, youth encouraged one another to read their writing to the rest of the class. Rather than devise systems to prevent students from sitting with their peers in class, I began encouraging them to do so, seeking out opportunities to build upon youth's peer relationships in support of their successful engagement with course curriculum. I spoke to them about the importance of encouraging their peers as we worked together toward reaching our collaborative goal of academic achievement and college access for all students.

I now try as often as possible to create opportunities for youth to work within self-selected peer groups, speaking explicitly with students about how and why I am expecting them to work productively in small groups of their choosing, while forefronting notions of culturally relevant peer interactions. These interactions draw upon notions of academic achievement, cultural competence, and sociopolitical awareness to support youth in creating peer relationships that encourage their engagement in college-going processes. A multimedia project documenting a class trip to a local college campus serves as an example. For the project, youth were asked to form small self-selected peer groups, raise questions about engaging in college-going processes, attend a class trip to a local college campus where they could ask their questions, and utilize digital media to document their experiences (Marciano, 2011). Youth later worked collaboratively within their groups to create 3- to 5-minute-long multimedia projects that set the digital photographs and videos they took on the trip to music, focusing on answering the questions they raised during the campus visit. Not only did the youth peer groups support one another's academic achievement by engaging in the curricular aspects of the project, but they demonstrated cultural competence in creating a multimedia project that would gain the interest of their peers. Further, youth demonstrated sociopolitical awareness by choosing to share their projects with peers who did not have access to the campus visit themselves.

Yet, youth are not always enrolled in classes with those they consider friends. Thus, I also aim to provide opportunities for youth to engage in curricular experiences with friends who may be enrolled in other sections of the course I teach. I return to the college tour media project as an example. Several of the youth chose to create working groups with friends who were enrolled in another section of the class. Because several of the classes I taught visited the college campus together, youth were not bound by the borders that can arise between students enrolled in different sections of the same course. Further, youth who frequently spent time with one another outside of school were able to work collaboratively on their projects outside of class, experiencing opportunities to use their leisure time together to complete their coursework. Many more opportunities exist to support youth in engaging in college-going processes through explicit discussions with other students about how and why culturally relevant peer interactions may facilitate the ways in which they share information about preparing for, applying to, and enrolling in college.

Questions and Actions for Individuals

1. How did your peers influence you at various points in your life, including your engagement in college-going processes? How and why did you engage with some peers and not others? Did your peers influence you primarily in positive or negative ways, or some combination of both?

2. How do media portrayals of youth influence your perceptions of youth peer groups? What are some specific examples of television shows, movies, music videos, and so on, that feature youth peer groups? Do these representations accurately depict how and why youth peer groups interact in comparison with the peer groups you have observed in your work with youth? Why or why not?

3. Reflect on your own schooling experiences. In what ways did the curriculum and teaching reflect and build upon (or not) your interactions with peers to support your college readiness and access? Describe a time you were able to work with your peers on a curricular activity. What was the activity? How did engaging with your peers influence your engagement in the activity?

Questions and Actions for Small Groups
Within School Communities

1. How do you define the term *peer* in relation to the students with whom you work? What leads you to define the term *peer* in this way? What assumptions might you be making about peers in your definition? How might your definition of *peers* influence your interactions with youth?

2. In what ways are youth encouraged to collaborate with their peers as part of the official school curriculum? How do youth benefit from these collaborations? How might any challenges associated with encouraging peers to collaborate be addressed? How do these collaborations support youth's college readiness?

3. How might school personnel encourage youth to discuss their engagement in college-going processes with their peers in both formal and informal contexts? How might technology, including social media and student-created digital texts, be considered a resource for peer

collaboration and challenging inequitable access to college-going information?

Questions and Actions for Whole-School Communities

1.   What opportunities exist for students across grade levels to interact with one another (e.g., college fairs and college visits)? How might you incorporate digital literacies—such as seniors making videos about their experiences/insights engaging in college-going processes that could be shared with youth in the future—into the curriculum?
2.   How might the experiences of youth's peers outside of school be built upon in school contexts? How might youth's peers who do not attend the school be viewed as resources for sharing insight about college-going processes?
3.   What role might college students and alumni play in visiting current students to talk about their experiences that facilitated or hindered their applying to and attending college? How might their visits be incorporated into curriculum and pedagogical practices? What insight related to youth's race, ethnicity, socioeconomic status, age, and/or gender might be gained from youth's interactions with peers who have applied to and enrolled in college?

CHAPTER 7

Implications and Conclusion
Creating a Culturally Relevant, Schoolwide, College-Going Culture

Youth are making decisions for their futures embedded within the convergence of change in social, educational, cultural, and political realms of an increasingly highly technological, diverse, global society. Yet in the midst of this vast sea of change, the national high school graduation rates for Black and Latina/o youth have hovered around the 50% mark for many years, subsequently contributing to their low enrollment in a range of postsecondary institutions. These educational inequities have long-term consequences for youth's quality of life such as job security and health benefits as well as societal advancement, thereby calling for educators to pursue promising approaches to challenge these alarming trends. In response to this challenge, the purpose of our research has been to afford opportunities for 25 Black and Latina/o youth to provide first-person perspectives on the complexities of their daily lives and to illuminate some of the significant influences that have supported or hindered their college readiness and access.

We believe that students' perspectives of their experiences as college-bound youth and those of their families, teachers, administrators, and counselors play an important part in what we, as educators, do to create a culturally relevant, college-going high school culture. This culture reflects policies and practices that create accessibility for all students to information and resources that prepare youth to be college-ready, apply to, and enroll in a range of postsecondary institutions (Holland & Farmer-Hinton, 2009; McClafferty, McDonough, & Nunez, 2002).

The overarching goal of this book is to facilitate a sense of collective responsibility among educators, youth, and family members to create a culturally relevant, schoolwide, college-going culture to improve educational experiences and outcomes for Black and Latina/o youth (see Figure 7.1). In so doing, we extend traditional conceptions of college readiness and access that fail to adequately consider youth's cultural backgrounds and that focus solely on the role of guidance counselors in the college-going process.

Culturally relevant education recognizes, acknowledges, and utilizes students' identities, backgrounds, and experiences as meaningful sources for creating learning environments for college readiness and access. To that end, we argue that the three interrelated tenets of culturally relevant education—student learning and achievement, cultural competence, and critical awareness of educational inequities—can undergird the development and enactment of innovative policies and practices supportive of Black and Latina/o youth's college readiness and access.

STUDENT LEARNING AND ACHIEVEMENT: CREATING RIGOROUS AND RELEVANT POLICIES AND PRACTICES

As we have discussed throughout this text, creating rigorous and relevant academic preparation policies through the core curriculum and testing structures is essential for supporting students' learning and academic achievement. We argue that culturally relevant education supports a climate of valuing and utilizing students' culture, which is fostered in the school and

Figure 7.1. Creating a Culturally Relevant, Schoolwide, College-Going Culture

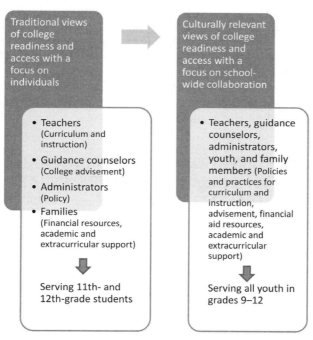

classrooms as a bridge between students' academic learning and their prior understandings, knowledge, and experiences. Educators learn from and about their students' cultures to make curriculum, instruction, and the creation of structures within schools meaningful by integrating these cultures into the policies and practices of the school. Culturally relevant policies and practices are demonstrated within the varied school structures as consistently clear messages of high expectations and standards of achievement for all youth as college bound; for example, in the school's mission statements and the "college talk" found within supportive relationships between youth and educators.

We also put forth that teachers, counselors, and administrators must move past traditional notions of college readiness as distinct from classroom practices in order to best facilitate youth's navigation of college-going processes. A culturally relevant and rigorous academic curriculum that builds upon the Common Core State Standards (2011) and students' cultures challenges youth, for example, to understand the central themes of a text and analyze its development; summarize the key supporting details and ideas; as well as integrate and evaluate content presented in diverse media and formats. Understanding the interrelated nature of the Common Core State Standards and students' cultures provides only one, albeit significant, entry point to college access. For Black and Latina/o youth, particularly those who are the first in their families to attend college, curricular connections to youth's cultural and historical backgrounds are a necessary component of college readiness. Classroom projects that incorporate culturally relevant texts for many Latina/o youth, such as *In the Time of the Butterflies* by Julia Alvarez, or that build upon youth's out of school engagement with digital and social media, not only challenge youth to meet the academic standards put forth by the Common Core State Standards (2011) but build upon youth's cultural knowledge to facilitate their academic learning.

SCHOOL STAFFS' AND YOUTH'S CULTURAL COMPETENCE: COMPLICATING CULTURE AND "FIXED" (RACIAL) IDENTITIES

While it is vital for educators to provide culturally relevant and rigorous academic preparation, it is not sufficient by itself as a change effort to effectively support Black and Latina/o youth's college readiness and access. Instead, we suggest that understanding the significant role of race and cultural backgrounds in the lives of youth and in their relationships with school staff is another essential element for facilitating youth's college readiness. Limiting the focus of college readiness solely to curricular change efforts lends itself to easily leaving unexamined the significant role of race and cultural backgrounds in the daily lives of youth and school staff. Black and Latina/o youth's experiences of schooling and the influences on their college-going processes contribute to understandings of the complexity of their social identities and the needed multidimensional images of them as academically excellent and culturally proficient. Moreover, for the past decade, changing demographic shifts have revealed an overwhelmingly White teaching, counseling, and administrative staff, and an increasingly diverse student population throughout our nation's schools. Yet, all staff may not have had opportunities to interact with and learn from people who are different from themselves, including but not limited to ethnicity, socioeconomic, or (dis)ability status. We argue that teachers, counselors, and administrators must be willing to develop the cultural competence and skills that value and utilize Black and Latina/o youth's backgrounds to create a culturally relevant approach to their identities that support youth's college readiness and access. More specifically, educators need to be willing to analyze their own identities, the daily lives and experiences of the youth whom they serve, the policies and practices within their schools, and the relationships among these overlapping experiences and perspectives. In so doing, culturally competent educators may provide learning opportunities that support youth's maintenance of their cultural identities and the pursuit of academic excellence simultaneously.

Just as the 25 Black and Latina/o youth in our study offered insight into the multiplicity of their intersecting academic and cultural identities, so too can the youth with whom all educators work. By valuing the experiences, cultural knowledges, and backgrounds that exist within and across groups of both students and school staff, educators may better understand and build upon the complexity of youth's experiences rather than accepting a "fixed" cultural identity. For example, analyses of student academic performance and involvement in extracurricular activities aggregated by race, ethnicity, and/or gender can provide insight into which students are successfully negotiating school policies and practices, and which students may need more support to do so. Schools also can engage students in dialogue through surveys and focus group interviews to ask them to choose or recommend extracurricular activities and courses they want to access at school. Student choice creates a sense of relevance and belonging, thereby highlighting the potential for increased student engagement in school learning.

CRITICAL AWARENESS OF COLLEGE READINESS AND ACCESS: RECOGNIZING AND CHALLENGING EDUCATIONAL INEQUITIES

The development of a critical consciousness for both school staff and students in regard to the structures within schools and society that facilitate and/or hinder college readiness and access for Black and Latina/o youth is the third essential tenet undergirding culturally relevant education and college access. Culturally relevant educators are aware of the role they play individually and collectively in supporting or hindering youth's college readiness within schools. They not only are aware of but act upon school structures that disproportionately limit youth's educational experiences and outcomes, making students aware of such structures and encouraging them to take action as well. For example, youth co-researcher projects facilitate awareness of how peers are successfully negotiating (or not) school structures. Such projects may further support youth's culturally relevant peer interactions, developing a community of learners. This navigation of the college admissions process within cross-age peer structures in and outside of school affords opportunities for centering youth's experiences and challenging societal inequities.

Further, timing and planning for admission to a range of colleges is necessary beginning as early as 9th grade, and, in many cases, addressing this challenge requires altering current or creating new structures within schools. For example, 9th-grade orientation sessions can move beyond the sole purpose of transitioning students into high school. They can serve as a more culturally relevant school structure that provides opportunities to immediately encourage all students to consider college as an option and to prepare them to make informed plans to be college-ready. Sharing information with youth about the percentages of Black and Latina/o youth who are graduating from high school and attending college, as well as information about those who are successfully negotiating structures within their own schools, also may develop a critical awareness among youth. Such an awareness can assist youth in seeing that their educational attainment is part of a broader sociohistorical context, one that may be explicitly identified and challenged.

TOWARD A SCHOOLWIDE, CULTURALLY RELEVANT, COLLEGE-GOING CULTURE

School reform efforts targeting culturally relevant education and college access can support educators, youth, and their families in critical collaboration to enact change in the policies and practices of curriculum and teaching, organizational structures, and professional development within schools (see Figure 7.2). The existing educational inequity in college readiness for Black and Latina/o youth is not going to be remedied solely through the development of more rigorous academic curricula, such as those informed by the

Common Core State Standards (2011), or other curricular changes. Rather, it is through the actions of those who are prepared to engage in critical reflection of their own identities and school contexts, including organizational structures, that the reform efforts needed to prepare all youth to apply for and to enroll in college will be enacted. These actions recognize and build on youth's cultural backgrounds and experiences to ensure that youth have access to learning opportunities that engage them in a college preparatory curriculum, support their cultural identities, and strengthen their critical awareness of college readiness.

Figure 7.2. Creating a Culturally Relevant, Schoolwide, College-Going Culture for Black and Latina/o Youth

Culturally relevant tenets*	Beliefs, norms and values	Policies and practices	Examples
Student learning and achievement: Creating rigorous and relevant policies and practices	High expectations that youth in grades 9–12 are college bound	Curriculum: Aligning curricular standards with culturally relevant resources	Analyzing Alvarez's *In the Time of the Butterflies*, making connections to youth's perspectives
School staff and youth's cultural competence: Complicating culture and fixed (racial) identities	The role of culture in relationships between youth and school staff is important	Extracurricular activities: Involving youth in deciding which activitites are offered and when	Survey incoming 9th-graders; facilitate informal activities such as lunch Yu-Gi-Oh club
Sociopolitical awareness: Developing an understanding of inequality in college readiness and access	Educators and youth collaborate to address inequities in college readiness and access	Explicitly discussing college readiness and access inequities with students	Youth co-researcher projects explore peers' negotiations of college going

*While the culturally relevant tenets +are separated into distinct categories for purposes of illustrating specific examples of each, we recognize that the tenets work together and inform one another to create a schoolwide, college-going culture.

Graduation Rate, Class of 2009
Intersection: Gender and Race/Ethnicity

Students	National	CA*	NM	NY
FEMALE				
American Indian/Alaska Native	56.1	NA	51.5	61.5
Asian/Pacific Islander	81.5	89.5	67.2	85
Black	65.3	61.1	39.3	61
Hispanic	66.1	64.1	67.5	61.2
White	80.2	86	58.8	85.5
MALE				
American Indian/Alaska Native	49.6	NA	45.5	46.8
Asian/Pacific Islander	79.2	83.5	72.9	78.5
Black	51.9	48.8	30.5	53.3
Hispanic	58.1	53.9	56.6	53.3
White	76.1	79.8	50.5	81.5

In percentages; Editorial Projects in Education Research Center, 2012.

Source: Statistics for California represent the class of 2008, the most recent year for which data are available; Editorial Projects in Education Research Center, 2011.

APPENDIX B

Ethnographic Context and Youth Co-Researcher Methodology

The inclusion and analyses of Black and Latina/o youth's interpretations of systemic schoolwide reform efforts can inform and shape youth-oriented policies, practices, and structures to promote retention in high school and more equitable access to a range of postsecondary institutions. Several studies analyzing youth's college-going processes have been limited to surveys, longitudinal questionnaires, or qualitative methods to research youth's college choice and access during their senior year (Horvatt, 1996; McDonough, 1997; Tierney, 2009). While informative, these methodologies do not adequately address the structures of power, cultural values, and practices that shape and are shaped within negotiations of youth's college-going processes in 9th–12th grades. We utilize conventional and innovative ethnographic methods, including a youth co-researcher methodology, to document and analyze the findings of two central research questions:

1. What factors in and out of a college-focused high school influence Black and Latina/o youth's understanding of college-going processes?
2. How do Black and Latina/o youth negotiate these influences on their college-going processes?

The overarching goal is to document the independent and interacting factors influencing Black and Latina/o youth's understandings of college-going processes in order to improve their educational experiences and to ensure greater access to postsecondary institutions.

Researchers working within critical frameworks consider critical ethnography as one of the most important methodologies for using research tools that allow the examination and transformation of educational and social inequalities (Foley, Levinson, & Hurtig, 2001; Luttrell, 2009; Villenas & Dehyle, 1999). Critical ethnography is particularly salient to our research, providing a methodology for unearthing and transforming educational inequities faced by Black and Latina/o youth and their families in negotiating college-going processes in under-resourced high schools. Important goals of this critical ethnographic study utilizing feminist theoretical lenses were: (1)

to center the perspectives of youth as important stakeholders in the school reform process; (2) to illuminate how youth employ their agency in interpreting and negotiating college-going processes (Delgado Bernal, 1998); (3) to challenge linear assumptions of youth development and transitions such as those from high school to college by addressing how youth's identities and negotiations of the college-going processes are shaped by their lives in multiple overlapping contexts such as school, media, and their futures (Fordham, 1996; Wyn, 2000); and (4) to recommend more equitable high school policies and practices to facilitate youth's college access.

The research team moved to include a youth co-researcher methodology to complement traditional ethnographic methods (Cook-Sather, 2002; Eisenhart, 2001; Knight, Dixon, Norton, & Ewald, 2003; Marciano & Watson, 2011; Morrell, 2004). The shift to a youth co-researcher methodology represents an activist-oriented framework with and by participants that is more culturally responsive to the unique characteristics of predominantly working class, Latina/o and Black family and community research paradigms in urban contexts (Cammarota & Fine, 2008; Mullings, 2000; Pizzaro, 1998). Embedded within the youth co-researcher methodology is an epistemological standpoint wherein the changing power dynamics in the research process unearth the role and use of knowledge production as part of the methodology and ways of writing about parents/family members and peer involvement with youth and the college-going process (Boudin & Knight, 2006; Knight, Norton, Dixon, & Ewald, 2003). We draw on youth's agency to name, critically read, question, and act on the world around them for their futures and, more specifically, for understanding and benefiting from policies and practices that would facilitate their access to a range of colleges. In what follows, we briefly introduce Evergreen High School (Chapter 1 explains the college-focused structures of the school in more detail). Then, we describe the participants, selection criteria, and data collection methods and analysis that focus on the 9th- and 10th-grade years of a larger 4-year study, as these are the years that are missing in much of the literature on college readiness and access. First, we briefly describe our own professional and personal positionalities, which influenced our interest in college readiness and access.

Positionality

It is important to note our own positionalities as researchers in relation to the study. Michelle's interest in preparing educators as transformative leaders in schools and communities was strongly influenced by her participation with children and youth in varied learning communities such as Big Sister programs and learning (dis)abled programs in the Amish community in Pennsylvania. More specifically, while serving as a teacher and college advisor of racially, culturally, and linguistically diverse youth in urban schools in Oakland, California, she attempted to change many of the educational inequities they encountered. Over the years, the pervasiveness of inequitable educational policies and practices continuously has led Michelle to question and challenge her roles and responsibilities as a teacher educator and researcher. In so doing, Michelle seeks to enact practices that build the capacity of youth, teachers, administrators, counselors, and family members to work individually and collectively for improved educational and social experiences for youth, their families, and communities.

Joanne's desire to create equitable educational opportunities for youth stems from her experiences as a newspaper reporter, interacting within and writing about urban, suburban, and rural school communities across New York, New Jersey, and Rhode Island. Unsettled by the inequities she encountered in these contexts, often influenced by issues of race, ethnicity, and socioeconomic status of students and their families, Joanne sought to gain a deeper understanding of educational (in)opportunities and to enact change. She enrolled in an alternative teaching certification program, began teaching in an urban public school, and became a member of a collaborative school community where teachers, guidance counselors, and school administrators work together toward youth's academic achievement and college access. Joanne's work as an educator, doctoral student, and researcher continues to be shaped by the multiple perspectives of youth and their families as she strives to influence educational policies and practices that lead toward improved educational opportunities and possibilities.

Together, Michelle and Joanne see the potential of conducting research with, for, and by youth to better understand how their perspectives can affect school reform efforts to create more equitable opportunities that enrich their lives.

Research Site

The multicultural university research team, consisting of an African American professor and five graduate students, two Black, one Latina, two White, and one Asian, conducted a critical ethnography at Evergreen High School in New York City. This comprehensive high school was engaged in college-focused reform efforts. Additionally, 25 Black and Latina/o youth from Evergreen High School acted as co-researchers. Many of these youth and their families chose Evergreen because of its excellent academic and extracurricular reputation. As a school of "choice," Evergreen receives 50% more applications than its neighboring high school. Located in a predominantly Latina/o and Black under-resourced urban community, poor and working class Black and Latina/o students constitute more than 90% of the

3,500 student body. Additionally, 43% are males and 57% are females. The school is staffed by two schoolwide college counselors, ten guidance counselors, more than 300 teachers, and 11 administrators. While the school reports that over 90% of its students go on to college, there is differential emphasis on college preparation within and among ten small learning houses. Of the ten houses, the general and health careers houses have the lowest numbers of students going on to college. In order to gain insights into how the school could address this disparity, administrators entered into a research partnership with Teachers College, Columbia University.

Participants

The primary participants were 25 predominantly working class, Black and Latina/o youth who were selected by a "community nomination" process (Ladson-Billings, 1994a). The nomination process involved asking 9th-grade teachers, counselors, administrators, parents, students, and security guards after the first 2 months of school to create a list of ten college-bound students whom they believed fit the following criteria: students in the general or medical careers house, Black and Latina/o youth from under-resourced urban communities (regardless of grade point average), and students involved in multiple activities such as child care, work, or extracurricular activities. All 25 of the students were nominated and voluntarily participated. Thirteen of the youth are male and 12 are female. Seventeen participants self-identify as Black, Ghanaian, or Jamaican, and eight as Puerto Rican or Dominican. At least one of each student's participating teachers, counselors, administrators, or family members also was individually interviewed for 30–45 minutes, for a total of 61 participants.

Individual and Focus Group Interviews

Students participated in two interviews each year, one individual interview at the beginning of the year and one focus group interview at the end of the year, to share their perspectives of the college-going processes influencing them. Interviews lasted from 30 to 45 minutes and took place in an office or classroom at the school site. Interviews were semistructured to ensure that specific topics, such as parent/family involvement, peer support, literacy, and culturally relevant teaching practices, were covered. Youth participated in videotaped focus groups for 30–45 minutes during their lunch period from 9th to 11th grade. We probed for specificity around the ways youth named familial support, identified family involvement in their college decision-making processes, and negotiated conflicting perspectives around their college-going identities from schools, peers, and families. Youth also provided member checks within the group interviews by clarifying analyses of emerging themes based on the topics raised in individual interviews and informed socially constructed meanings of the college-going process through students' interactions with peers.

Observations and Written Documentation

The research team observed school activities for 2–3 days a week to examine the broader school culture and college-going structures, including college fairs, extracurricular activities, and counseling procedures, in the context of school-centered, college-focused reform efforts. All 25 youth were observed in at least one of their classes, lunch time, free periods, and extracurricular activities during 9th and 10th grades. Two participants left the school before the completion of the study. The team completed fieldnotes after the observations. We also collected written documentation about the goals and objectives of the schoolwide college-focused reform efforts, such as school policies, college preparation materials, and instructional lessons.

Youth Co-Researcher Methodology

A youth co-researcher methodology emphasizes the ways that Black and Latina/o youth reveal they are holders, constructors, and negotiators of knowledge surrounding their families and peers' involvement in their college-going processes (Delgado Bernal, 1998), while simultaneously supporting their agency, empowerment, and critical literacies as college-bound youth (Knight, Dixon, Norton, & Bentley, 2006). The youth co-researchers interviewed family members who supported them in their college-going processes and older peers who could share about their own college-going processes.

Participating youth in 9th grade attended a 45-minute videotaped training session in small groups of three to six in which the research team shared their experiences of having interviewed a parent using the given protocol of questions, familiarized students with the interview protocol, and answered all questions. Youth were provided with the eight-question protocol constructed by the research team. They were asked to choose five of the eight questions and to create two or more of their own to use in the interview process. Smaller group research training sessions took place, including practice in interviewing and helping youth to construct additional questions. Some of the questions included: (1) How do you think Evergreen supports me going to college? (2) In what ways do you support me going to college? and (3) Are you saying that most people expect less of Black and minority families because of where they grew up? Finally, each youth received a tape recorder, a notebook, and the interview protocol, with space for them to write the two to three additional questions, and information on obtaining permission to record and publish the data, while ensuring anonymity. They engaged reflexively through written or audiotaped journals to examine their critical literacies and agencies around the process and content of the interviews. All interviews were transcribed upon receipt. During follow-up meetings, Black and Latina/o youth co-researchers engaged in collective reflexivity with research. A similar process took place in 10th and 11th grades with youth co-researchers in interviewing their peers.

Data Analysis

The authors analyzed data utilizing themes from the literature on college preparation and access as well as the tenets and underpinning of culturally relevant theory. Participant responses were coded for the themes that emerged around such issues as future aspirations, college choices, student relationships, test preparation, extracurricular activities, as well as student learning, achievement, cultural competence, and critical consciousness. Youth also provided member checks in individual and focus group interviews. Moreover, research committed to social change and to dismantling inequitable structures must have accountability measures to ensure the trustworthiness or rigor and relevance of the data. These measures include triangulation of data collection methods and construct validity.

Future Directions

Our research has illustrated the ways in which individuals and schools can begin to create policies and practices to support a schoolwide, culturally relevant, college-going culture for Black and Latina/o youth. The findings serve as a starting point for identifying some of the factors influencing the college readiness and access of the Black and Latina/o youth in our study. Additional culturally relevant factors specific to particular school contexts may be added over time to build a more robust understanding of policies and practices beneficial to youth. Mixed-methods studies that incorporate quantitative data, such as the high school graduation and college access rates of youth, and qualitative methodologies that explore the complex perspectives and realities of youth's lives, also are needed to provide broad understandings of contextual factors that influence youth's college readiness and access.

Within our research study, we also employed a youth co-researcher methodology as a deliberate choice to enhance youth's academic research skills and increase their access to culturally relevant information about college through interviews with family members and peers. Given the increasing role of technology in the lives of youth, we argue that future research methodologies that incorporate youth as co-researchers build upon youth's engagement of social media and technology, which may provide further insight into how to best support the culturally relevant college readiness and access of youth.

References

Allen, K., Jackson, I., & Knight, M. (2012). Complicating culturally relevant pedagogy: Unpacking African immigrants cultural identities. *International Journal of Multicultural Education, 14*(2), 1–28.

Alvarez, J. (1994). *In the time of the butterflies*. Chapel Hill, NC: Algonquin Books of Chapel Hill.

Auerbach, S. (2004). Engaging Latino parents in supporting college pathways: Lessons from a college access program. *Journal of Hispanic Higher Education, 3*(2), 125–145.

Bedolla, L. G. (2010). Good ideas are not enough: Considering the politics underlying students' postsecondary transitions. *Journal of Education for Students Placed At Risk, 15*(1), 9–26.

Bonous-Hammarth, M., & Allen, W. R. (2004). A dream deferred: The critical factor of timing in college preparation and outreach. In W. G. Tierney, Z. B. Corwin, & J. E. Colyar (Eds.), *Preparing for college: Nine elements of effective outreach* (pp. 155–172). Albany, NY: State University of New York Press.

Boudin, K., & Knight, M. (2006, April). *Can peers make a difference? Urban youth co-researchers use participatory research, strengthening their college-going process*. Paper presented at the annual meeting of the American Educational Research Association, San Francisco, CA.

Brown, R., & Evans, W. P. (2002). Extracurricular activity and ethnicity: Creating greater school connection among diverse student populations. *Urban Education, 37*(1), 41–58.

Buendia, E. (2010). Reconsidering the urban in urban education: Interdisciplinary conversations. *Urban Review, 43*(1), p. 1–21.

Cammarota, J & Fine, M. (Eds.) (2008). *Revolutionizing education: Youth participatory action research in motion*. New York: Teachers College Press.

Casillas, D. (2012). Taking count of gender and legal status within Latino media policy. In P. Noguera, A. Hurtado, & E. Fergus (Eds.), *Invisible no more: Understanding the disenfranchisement of Latino men and boys* (pp. 122–135). New York: Routledge.

Center for Higher Education Policy Analysis. (n.d.). *The impact of peers on college preparation: A review of the literature*. Retrieved from http://www.uscrossier. org/pullias/wp-content/uploads/2012/02/CHEPA_The_Impact_of_Peers_on_College_Preparation.pdf

Choy, S. P., Horn, L. J., Nunez, A., & Chen, X. (2000). Transition to college: What helps at-risk students and students whose parents did not attend college. *New Directions for Institutional Research, 107*, 45–63.

City University of New York. (2011). CAT FAQs. Retrieved from http://www. cuny.edu/academics/testing/cuny-assessment-tests/faqs.html#2

Cochran-Smith, M., Davis, D., & Fries, M. K. (2003). Multicultural teacher education: Research, practice and policy. In J. Banks (Ed.), *Handbook of research on multicultural education* (2nd ed., pp. 747–759). San Francisco: Jossey-Bass.

Common Application. (2012). Retrieved from https://www.commonapp.org/ CommonApp/Docs/DownloadForms/2012/2012PacketFY_download.pdf

Common Core State Standards. (2011). Retrieved from http://www.corestandards. org/assets/CCSSI_ELA%20Standards.pdf

Cook-Sather, A. (2002). Authorizing students' perspectives: Toward trust, dialogue, and change in education. *Educational Researcher, 31*(4), 3–14.

Corwin, Z. B., Colyar, J. E., & Tierney, W. G. (2005). Introduction: Engaging research and practice—extracurricular and curricular influences on college access. In W. G. Tierney, Z. B. Corwin, & J. E. Colyar (Eds.), *Preparing for college: Nine elements of effective outreach* (pp. 1–12). Albany, NY: State University of New York Press.

Corwin, Z. B., & Tierney, W. (2007). *Getting there and beyond.* Los Angeles: Center for Higher Education Policy Analysis.

Datnow, A., Solorzano, D. G., Watford, T., & Park, V. (Eds.). (2010). Pathways to postsecondary education and beyond: Maximizing opportunities for youth in poverty. *Journal of Education for Students Placed At Risk, 15*(1–2).

De Gaetano, Y., Williams, L. R., & Volk, D. (1998). *Kaleidoscope: A multicultural approach for the primary school classroom.* New York: Teachers College Press.

Dei, G., Mazzuca, J., & McIssac, E. (1997). *Reconstructing "dropout": A critical ethnography of the dynamics of Black students' disengagement from school.* Toronto, Canada: University of Toronto Press.

Delgado Bernal, D. (1998). Using a Chicana feminist epistemology in educational research. *Harvard Education Review, 68*(4), 555–582.

Delgado Bernal, D., Aleman, E., & Carmona, J. (2008). Transnational and transgenerational Latina/o cultural citizenship among kindergarteners, their parents, and university students in Utah. *Social Justice, 35*(1), 28–46.

Dutro, E., Kazemi, E., Balf, R., & Yin-Sheue, L. (2008). "What are you and where are you from?": Race, identity, and the vicissitudes of cultural relevance. *Urban Education, 43*(3), 269–300.

Dylan, S. (2010, August 25). Eastern states dominate in winning school grants. *The New York Times,* p. A3.

Editorial Projects in Education Research Center and *Education Week.* (2011). *Diplomas Count 2011: Beyond high school, before baccalaureate: Meaningful alternatives to a four-year degree.* Bethesda, MD: Editorial Projects in Education Inc.

Editorial Projects in Education Research Center and *Education Week*. (2012). *Diplomas Count 2012: Trailing behind, moving forward: Latino students in U.S. Schools*. Bethesda, MD: Editorial Projects in Education Inc.

Edmonds, T. (2008). *College Hill Atlanta* [Television series]. New York: BET.

Eisenhart, M. (2001). Educational ethnography past, present, and future: Ideas to think with. *Educational Researcher, 30*(8), 16–27.

El Nassar, H., & Overberg, P. (2010, August 27). Kindergartens see more Hispanic, Asian students. *USA Today*, p. A1.

Evergreen High School.(n.d.). *Student/parent handbook and course catalogue.*

Falchuk, B. (Writer), & Buecker, B. (Director). (2010). Never been kissed [Television series episode]. In R. Murphy, B. Falchuk, I. Brennan, & D. Di Loreto (Producers), *Glee*. Los Angeles, CA: Fox Broadcasting.

Farmer-Hinton, R. (2006). On becoming college prep: Examining the challenges charter school staff members face while executing a school's mission. *Teachers College Record, 108*(6), 1214–1240.

Farmer-Hinton, R., & McCullough, R. G. (2008). College counseling in charter high schools: Examining the opportunities and challenges. *The High School Journal, 91*(4), 77–90.

Fisherkeller, J. (1997). Everyday learning about identities among young adolescents in television culture. *Anthropology & Education Quarterly 28*, 467–492.

Flanagan, C., Levine, P., & Settersten, R. (2011). *Civic engagement and the changing transition to adulthood*. Medford, MA: Tufts University, Center for Information and Research on Civic Learning and Engagement.

Flores-Gonzalez, N. (2002). *School kids/Street kids: Identity development in Latino students*. New York: Teachers College Press.

Foley, D., Levinson, B., & Hurtig, J. (2001). Anthropology goes inside: The new educational ethnography of ethnicity and gender. In W. Secada (Ed.), *Review of research in education*, (pp. 37–98). Washington, DC: American Educational Research Association.

Fordham, S. (1996). *Blacked out: Dilemmas of race, identity, and success at Capitol High*. Chicago: University of Chicago Press.

Gándara, P. (2002). A study of high school Puente: What we have learned about preparing Latino youth for postsecondary education. *Educational Policy, 16*(4), 474–495.

Gándara, P., & Contreras, F. (2009). *The Latino education crisis: The consequences of failed social policies*. Cambridge, MA: Harvard University Press.

Gay, G. (2010). *Culturally responsive teaching: Theory, research, and practice*. New York: Teachers College Press.

Gee, J. P. (2007). *What video games have to teach us about learning and literacy*. New York: Palgrave Macmillan.

Gibson, M., Gándara, P., & Koyama, J. (2004). *School connections: U.S. Mexican youth, peers, and school achievement*. New York: Teachers College Press.

Gildersleeve, R. E. (2010). Access between and beyond borders. *Journal of College Admission*, pp. 3–10.

Godinez, F. (2006). Haciendo que hacer: Braiding cultural knowledge into educational practices and policies. In D. Delgado Bernal, C. Elenes, F. Godinez, & S. Villenas (Eds.), *Chicana/Latina education in everyday life: Feminist perspectives on pedagogy and epistemology* (pp. 25–38). New York: State University of New York Press.

Gonzalez, K, Jovel, J., & Stoner, C. (2004). Latinas: The new Latino majority in college. *New Directions for Student Services, 105*, 17–27.

Gonzalez, K., Stoner, C., & Jovel, J. (2003). Examining the role of social capital in access to college for Latinas: Toward a college opportunity framework. *Journal of Hispanic Higher Education, 2*, 146–170.

Goodwin, L. (2010). Globalization and the preparation of quality teachers: Rethinking knowledge domains for teaching. *Teaching Education, 21*, 19–32.

Guest, A., & Schneider, B. (2003). Adolescents' extracurricular participation in context: The mediating effects of school, communities, and identity. *Sociology of Education, 76*(2), 89–109.

Hearn, J, & Holdsworth, J. (2005). Cocurricular activities and students' college prospects: Is there a connection? In W. G. Tierney, Z. B. Corwin, & J. E. Colyar (Eds.), *Preparing for college: Nine elements of effective outreach* (pp. 135–154). Albany, NY: State University of New York Press.

Hobbs, R. (2010). *Digital and media literacy: A plan of action*. White paper on the digital and media literacy recommendations of the Knight Commission on the information needs of communities in a democracy. Washington, DC: The Aspen Institute.

Holland, A., & Andre, T. (1987). Participation in extracurricular activities in secondary school: What is known, what needs to be known? *Review of Educational Research, 57*(4), 437–466.

Holland, N., & Farmer-Hinton, R. (2009). Leave no school behind: The importance of a college culture in urban public high schools. *The High School Journal, 92*(3), 24–43.

Hollins, E., & Torres-Guzman, M. E. (2005). Research on preparing teachers for diverse populations. In M. K. Cochran-Smith & K. Zeichner (Eds.), *Studying teacher education: The report of the AERA Panel on Research and Teacher Education* (pp. 477–548). Mahwah, NJ: Lawrence Erlbaum Associates.

Holloway, J. H. (2002). Extracurricular activities and student motivation. *Educational Leadership, 60*(1), 80–81.

Horn, C. (2003). High-stakes testing and students: Stopping or perpetuating a cycle of failure? *Theory Into Practice, 42*(1), 30–41.

Horvat, E. M. (1996, April). *Structure, standpoint, and practices: The construction and meaning of the boundaries of Blackness for African-American female high school seniors in the college choice process*. Paper presented at the annual meeting of the American Educational Research Association, Chicago, IL.

Hossler, D., & Gallagher, K. (1987). Studying college student choice: A three-phase model and the implications for policy makers. *College and University, 62*, 207–221.

Howard, T. (2001). Telling their side of the story. African-American students' perceptions of culturally relevant teaching. *The Urban Review, 33*(2), 131–149.

Howard, T. (2010). Who really cares? The disenfranchisement of African American males in PreK–12 schools: A critical race theory perspective. *Teachers College Record, 110*(5), 954–985.

Hubbard, L., & Mehan, H. (1999). Race and reform: Educational "niche picking" in a hostile environment. *The Journal of Negro Education, 68*(2), 213–226.

Hurtado, A. (2003). Theory in the flesh: Toward an endarkened epistemology. *Qualitative Studies in Education, 16*(2), 215–225.

Jarsky, K., McDonough, P., & Nunez, A. (2009). Establishing a college culture in secondary schools through P–20 collaboration: A case study. *Journal of Hispanic Higher Education, 8*(4), 357–373.

Jewitt, C. (2005). Multimodality, "reading," and "writing" for the 21st century. *Discourse: Studies in the Cultural Politics of Education, 26*(3), 315–331.

Jordan, W., & Cooper, R. (2003). High school reform and Black male students: Limits and possibilities of policy and practice. *Urban Education, 38*(2), 196–216.

Jun, A., & Colyar, J. (2002). Parental guidance suggested: Family in college preparation programs. In W. G. Tierney & L. S. Hagedorn (Eds.), *Increasing access to college: Extending possibilities for all students* (pp. 195–216). Albany, NY: State University of New York Press.

Kafia, Y., & Peppler, K. (2011). Youth, technology and DIY: Developing participatory competencies in creative media production. *Review of Research in Education, 35*, 89–119.

Kirst, M., & Venezia, A. (2004). *From high school to college.* San Francisco: Jossey-Bass.

Knight, M. (2003). Through urban youth's eyes: Negotiating K–16 policies, practices, and their futures. *Educational Policy, 17*, 531–557.

Knight, M. (2010). Enacting care, preparing for college and increasing access for Black youth. *Journal of Students Placed at Risk, 15*(2), 158–172.

Knight, M. (2011). "It's already happening": Learning from civically engaged transnational immigrant youth. *Teachers College Record, 113*(6), 1275–1292.

Knight, M., Dixon, I., Norton, N., & Bentley,C. (2006). Critical literacies as feminist affirmations and interventions: Contexualizing Latina youth's construction of their college-bound identities. In D. Delgado Bernal, C. Elenes, F. Godinez, & S. Villenas (Eds.), *Chicana/Latina education in everyday life: Feminist perspectives on pedagogy and epistemology* (pp. 39–58). Albany, NY: State University of New York Press.

Knight, M., Nixon, I., Norton, N., & Bentley, C. (2004). Extending learning communities: New technologies, multiple literacies, and culture blind pedagogies. *Urban Review, 36*(2), 101–118.

Knight, M., Norton, N., Bentley, C., & Dixon, I. (2004). The power of Black and Latina/o counterstories: Urban families and college-going processes. *Anthropology & Education Quarterly, 35*(1), 99–120.

Knight, M., & Oesterreich, H. (2002). (In)(Di)Visible youth identities: Insight from a feminist intersectional framework. In W. G. Tierney & L. S. Hagedorn (Eds.), *Increasing access to college: Extending possibilities for all students* (pp. 123–144). Albany, NY: State University of New York Press.

Knight, M., Oesterreich, H., & Newton, R. (2003). "It doesn't happen by accident": Creating successful cultures of college preparation for urban Latina/o youth. *Educators of Urban Minorities, 2*(2), 91–107.

Ladson-Billings, G. (1994a). *The dreamkeepers: Successful teachers of African American children*. San Francisco: Jossey-Bass.

Ladson-Billings, G. (1994b). What we can learn from multicultural education research. *Educational Leadership, 51*(8), 22–26.

Ladson-Billings, G. (1995). Toward a theory of culturally relevant pedagogy: *American Educational Research Journal, 32*(3), 465–491.

Ladson-Billings, G. (2001). *Crossing over to Canaan: The journey of new teachers in diverse classrooms*. San Francisco: Jossey-Bass.

Ladson-Billings, G. (2002). I ain't writin' nuttin': Permission to fail and demands to succeed in urban classrooms. In L. Delpit & J. Kilgour Dowdy (Eds.), *The skin that we speak: Thoughts on language and culture in the classroom* (pp. 107–120). New York: The New Press.

Latina Feminist Group. (2001). *Telling to live: Latina feminist testimonios*. Durham, NC: Duke University Press.

Lewis-Charp, H., Yu, H. C., & Friedlaender, D. (2004). The influence of intergroup relations on school engagement: Two cases. In M. A. Gibson, P. Gándara, & J. P. Koyama (Eds.), *School connections: U.S. Mexican youth, peers, and school achievement* (pp. 107–128). New York: Teachers College Press.

Lindsey, R. B.; Robins, K. N.; & Terrell, R. D. (2009). *Cultural proficiency: A manual for school leaders*. Thousand Oaks, CA: Corwin Press.

Lipman, P. (1996). The missing voice of culturally relevant teachers in school restructuring. *The Urban Review, 28*(1), 41–62.

Lopez, N. (2002). *Hopeful girls, troubled boys: Race and gender disparity in urban education*. New York: Routledge.

Loza, P. (2003). A system at risk: College outreach programs and the educational neglect of underachieving Latino high school students. *The Urban Review, 35*(1), 43–57.

Luttrell, W. (Ed.). (2009). *Qualitative educational research: Readings in reflexive methodology and transformative practice* (pp. 1–17). New York: Routledge.

Magolda, P. (2000). The campus tour ritual: Exploring community discourses in higher education. *Anthropology and Education Quarterly, 31*(1), 24–36.

Mallan, K., & Pearce, S. (2003). *Youth cultures: Texts, images, and identities.* Westport, CT: Praeger.

Marciano, J. (2004, April). *Creating community in schools.* Paper presented at the annual conference of the Center for Urban Education, Long Island University, Brooklyn, NY.

Marciano, J. (2005, March). *Creating community in the high school English classroom.* Paper presented at the conference of the New York City Teaching Fellows, Fellows at Five: Celebrating Accomplishments, Creating the Future, New York.

Marciano, J. (2011, November). *"It makes me wanna 'go hard'": Exploring positive peer partnerships in the literacy and college-going processes of youth.* Paper presented at the annual meeting of the National Council of Teachers of English, Chicago, IL.

Marciano, J., & Watson, V. W. M. (2011, November). *Toward possibilities and civic imaginaries—engaging ethnographic methods and (re)presentations with youth co-researchers: A literature review.* Paper presented at the annual meeting of the American Anthropological Association, Montreal, Canada.

Marsh, H., & Kleitman, S. (2002). Extracurricular school activities: The good, the bad, and the nonlinear. *Harvard Educational Review, 72*(4), 464–514.

Mazerella, M. (2011). *Mediated girlhood: New explorations of girls' media culture.* New York: Peter Lang.

McClafferty, K., McDonough, P., & Nunez, A. (2002, April). *What is college culture? Facilitating college preparation through organizational change.* Paper presented at the annual meeting of the American Educational Research Association, New Orleans, LA.

McDonough, P. (1997). *Choosing colleges: How social class and schools structure opportunity.* Albany, NY: State University of New York Press.

McDonough, P. (2005). Counseling matters: Knowledge, assistance, and organizational commitment in college preparation. In W. G. Tierney, Z. B. Corwin, & J. E. Colyar (Eds.), *Preparing for college: Nine elements of effective outreach* (pp. 69–87). Albany, NY: State University of New York Press.

McNally, A., & Safran, J. (Writers), & Buckley, N. (Director). (2008). New Haven can wait [Television series episode]. In J. Schwartz & S. Savage (Producers), *Gossip girl.* New York: The CW.

McNeal, R. B. (1998). High school extracurricular activities: Closed structures and stratifying patterns of participation. *The Journal of Educational Research, 91*, 183–191.

Media That Matters. (2012). Media That Matters film festival: Short films that inspire action. Retrieved from http://www.mediathatmattersfest.org/films

Mitchell, C. A., & Reid-Walsh, J. (Eds.). (2007). *Girl culture: An encyclopedia* (Vol. 1). Westport, CT: Greenwood.

Moll, L. C., Amanti, C., Neff, D., & Gonzalez, N. (1992). Funds of knowledge for teaching: Using a qualitative approach to connect homes and classrooms. *Theory Into Practice, 31*(2), 132–141.

Moll, L., & Gonzalez, N. (2001). Lessons from research with language-minority children. In E. Cushman, E. Kintgen, & B. Kroll (Eds.), *Literacy: A critical sourcebook* (pp. 156–171). Boston: Bedford/St. Martin's.

Montgomery, K., Gottlieb-Robles, B., & Larson, G. (2004). *Youth as e-citizens in a digital generation.* Washington, DC: American University, Center for Social Media School of Communications.

Moreno, J. (2002). The long-term outcomes of Puente. *Educational Policy, 16*(4), 572–587.

Morrell, E. (2004). *Becoming critical researchers: Literacy and empowerment for urban youth.* New York: Peter Lang.

Mullings, L. (2000). African American women making themselves: Notes on Black feminist research. *Souls, 2*(4), 18–29.

Natriello, G., & Pallas, A. M. (2001). The development and impact of high-stakes testing. In G. Orfield & M. L. Kornhaber (Eds.), *Raising standards or raising barriers? Inequality and high-stakes testing in public education* (pp. 19–38). New York: Century Foundation Press.

New York State Education Department (2012). The New York State school report card: Accountability and overview report 2010-2011. Retrieved from: https://reportcards.nysed.gov/files/2010-11/AOR-2011-331300010265.pdf

Noguera, P., Hurtado, A., & Fergus, E. (Eds.). (2012). *Invisible no more: Understanding the disenfranchisement of Latino men and boys.* New York: Routledge.

Oakes, J. (1987). Tracking in secondary schools: A contextual perspective. *Educational Psychologist, 22*(2), 129–153.

Oakes, J., Rogers, J., Lipton, M., & Morrell, E. (2002). The social construction of college access: Confronting the technical, cultural, and political barriers to low-income students of color. In W. G. Tierney & L. S. Hagedorn (Eds.), *Increasing access to college: Extending possibilities for all students* (pp. 105–121). Albany, NY: State University of New York Press.

Oakes, J., Wells, A. S., & Jones, M. (1997). Detracking: The social construction of ability, cultural politics, and resistance to reform. *Teachers College Record, 98*(3), 482–510.

O'Connor, C. (1999). Race, class, and gender in America: Narratives of opportunity among low-income African American youths. *Sociology of Education, 72*(3), 137–157.

Orfield, G., & Kornhaber, M. L. (2001). Preface. In G. Orfield & M. L. Kornhaber (Eds.), *Raising standards or raising barriers? Inequality and high-stakes testing in public education* (pp. ix–xii). New York: Century Foundation Press.

Perna, L., Rowan-Kenyon, H., Thomas, S., Anderson, R., & Li, C. (2008). The role of college counseling in shaping college opportunities: Variations across high schools. *The Review of Higher Education, 31*(2), 131–159.

Pizarro, M. (1998). Chicana/o power!: Epistemology and methodology for social justice and empowerment in Chicana/o communities. *International Journal of Qualitative Studies in Education,* 11, 57–80.

Quiroz, P. (2000). A comparison of organizational and cultural contexts of extracurricular participation and sponsorship in two high schools. *Educational Studies, 31*(3), 249–275.

Reid, K., & Knight, M. (2006). Disability for justification of exclusion of minorities: A critical history grounded in disability studies. *Educational Researcher, 35*(6), 18–24.

Rong, X. L., & Brown, F. (2001). The effects of immigrant generation and ethnicity on educational attainment among young African American and Caribbean Blacks in the United States. *Harvard Educational Review, 71*(3), 536–565.

Ryan, A. M. (2001). The peer group as a context for the development of young adolescent motivation and achievement. *Child Development, 72*(4), 1135–1150.

Sacks, P. (2007). *Tearing down the gates: Confronting the class divide in American education.* Berkeley: University of California Press.

Sanders, M. G. (1998). The effects of school, family, and community support on the academic achievement of African American adolescents. *Urban Education, 33*(3), 385–409.

Scribner, J. D., & Reyes, P. (1999). Creating learning communities for high-performing Hispanic students: A conceptual framework. In P. Reyes, J. D. Scribner, & A. P. Scribner (Eds.), *Lessons from high-performing Hispanic schools* (pp. 188–210). New York: Teachers College Press.

Shuford, B. (1998). Keeping the student-athlete on track. *Coach and Athletic Director, 67*, 4–5.

Siddle Walker, V., & Tompkins, R. H. (2004). Caring in the past: The case of a southern segregated African American school. In V. Siddle Walker & J. R. Snarey (Eds.), *Race-ing moral formation: African American perspectives on care and justice* (pp. 77–92). New York: Teachers College Press.

Simmons, R. (Producer). (2009). *Brave new voices* [Television series]. Hollywood, CA: HBO Home Video.

Simpson, D., & Bruckheimer, J. (Producers), & Smith, J. N. (Director). (1995). *Dangerous minds* [Motion picture]. Burbank, CA: Hollywood Pictures.

Sleeter, C. (2005). *Un-standardizing curriculum.* New York: Teachers College Press.

Sleeter, C., & Grant, C. A. (2009). *Making choices for multicultural education: Five approaches to race, class, and gender* (5th ed.). Hoboken, NJ: Wiley.

Smith, M. (2001). Low SES African American parents: Playing the college choice game on an unlevel field. *Journal of College Admission, 71*, 16–22.

Somers, P., Cofer, J., & VanderPutten, J. (2002). The early bird goes to college: The link between early college aspirations and postsecondary matriculation. *Journal of College Student Development, 43*(1), 93–99.

Stanton-Salazar, R. D., & Spina, S. U. (2005). Adolescent peer networks as a context for social and emotional support. *Youth & Society, 36*(4), 379–417.

Steinberg, J. (2010, March 2). Graduates fault advice of guidance counselors. *The New York Times*, p. A20.

Suskind, R. (1999). *A hope in the unseen*. New York: Broadway.

Thompson, A. (1998). Not the color purple: Black feminist lessons for educational caring. *Harvard Educational Review, 68*(4), 522–554.

Tierney, W. (2009). Applying to college. *Qualitative Inquiry, 15*(1), 79–95.

Tierney, W., & Auerbach, S. (2005). Toward developing an untapped resource: The role of families in college preparation. In W. G. Tierney, Z. B. Corwin, & J. E. Colyar (Eds.), *Preparing for college: Nine elements of effective outreach* (pp. 29–48). Albany, NY: State University of New York Press.

Tierney, W. G., & Colyar, J. E. (2005). The role of peer groups in college preparation programs. In W. G. Tierney, Z. B. Corwin, & J. E. Colyar (Eds.), *Preparing for college: Nine elements of effective outreach* (pp. 49–68). Albany, NY: State University of New York Press.

Tierney, W. G., Corwin, Z. B., & Colyar, J. E. (Eds.). (2005). *Preparing for college: Nine elements of effective outreach*. Albany, NY: State University of New York Press.

Tierney, W. G., & Hagedorn, L. S. (Eds.). (2002). *Increasing access to college: Extending possibilities for all students*. Albany, NY: State University of New York Press.

Tierney, W., & Venegas, K. (2009). Finding money on the table: Information, financial aid and access to college. *Journal of Higher Education, 80*(4), 363–388.

Tilman, L. (2006). Researching and writing from an African-American perspective: Reflective notes on three research studies. *International Journal of Qualitative Studies in Education, 19*(3), 265–287.

Trier, J. (2005). Sordid fantasies: Reading popular inner-city school films as racialized texts with pre-service teachers. *Race, Ethnicity, and Education, 8*(2), 171–189.

U.S. Census Bureau (2010). State & county quick facts: New Mexico. Retrieved from: http://quickfacts.census.gov/qfd/states/35000.html

U.S. Department of Education. (2009). National Center for Education Statistics. Retrieved from http://nces.ed.gov/fastFacts/display.asp?id=98

U.S. Department of Education. (2012). National Center for Education Statistics. Retrieved from http://nces.ed.gov/pubsearch/pubsinfo.asp?pubid=2012045

Valenzuela, A. (1999). *Subtractive schooling: U.S.–Mexican youth and the politics of caring*. Albany, NY: State University of New York Press.

Vasudevan, L. (2010). Education remix: New media, literacies, and the emerging digital geographies. *Digital Culture & Education, 2*(1), 62–82.

Villalpando, O., & Solorzano, D. (2005). The role of culture in college preparation programs: A review of the research literature. In W. G. Tierney, Z. B. Corwin,

& J. E. Colyar (Eds.), *Preparing for college: Nine elements of effective outreach* (pp. 13–28). Albany, NY: State University of New York Press.

Villenas, S., & Dehyle (1999). Critical race theory and ethnographies challenging the stereotypes: Latino families, schooling, resilience and resistance. *Curriculum Inquiry, 29*(4), 413–445.

Ware, F. (2006). Warm demander pedagogy: Culturally responsive teaching that supports a culture of achievement for African American students. *Urban Education, 41,* 427–457.

Waters, M. C. (1999). *Black identities: West Indian immigrant dreams and American realities.* Cambridge, MA: Harvard University Press.

Watt, K., Huerta, J., & Lozana, A. (2007). A comparison study of AVID and GEAR UP 10th grade students in two high schools in the Rio Grande Valley of Texas. *Journal of Education for Students Placed At Risk, 12*(2), 185–212.

Watt, K., Powell, C., & Mendiola, I. D. (2004). Implications of one comprehensive school reform model for secondary school students underrepresented in higher education. *Journal of Education for Students Placed At Risk, 9*(3), 241–259.

Weiler, J. (2000). *Codes and contradictions: Race, gender identity, and schooling.* Albany, NY: State University of New York Press.

Welch, O. M., & Hodges, C. R. (1997). *Standing outside on the inside: Black adolescents and the construction of academic identity.* Albany, NY: State University of New York Press.

Wright, B. (2011). I know who I am, do you? Identity and academic achievement of successful African-American male adolescents in an urban pilot high school in the United States. *Urban Education, 46*(4), 611–638.

Wyn, J. (2000, April). *Education for the new adulthood: Implications of youth research for education.* Paper presented at the annual meeting of the American Educational Research Association, New Orleans, LA.

Yonezawa, S., & Jones, M. (2009). Student voices: Generating reform from the inside out. *Theory Into Practice, 48,* 205–212.

Yosso, T. (2005). Whose culture has capital? A critical race theory discussion of community cultural wealth. *Race, Ethnicity and Education, 8*(1), 69–91.

Zumwalt, K., & Craig, E. (2005). Teachers' characteristics: Research on the demographic profile. In M. K. Cochran-Smith & K. Zeichner (Eds.), *Studying teacher education: The report of the AERA Panel on Research and Teacher Education* (pp. 111–156). Mahwah, NJ: Lawrence Erlbaum Associates.

Index

Notations of *t* or *f* next to a page denote table or figure respectively.

About the Authors

Michelle G. Knight is a professor at Teachers College, Columbia University, and a former middle school teacher and high school college advisor. Her work, funded by the National Academy of Education Spencer Postdoctoral Fellowship Program and the Spencer Foundation Small Research Grants Program, on Black and Latina/o youth's perspectives of college-going influences, has been published in *Educational Researcher, Urban Review, Qualitative Inquiry, Journal of Educational Policy, Journal of Education for Students Placed at Risk,* and *Journal of Education for Urban Minorities.*

Joanne E. Marciano is a doctoral student and research associate at Teachers College, Columbia University, and a high school English teacher. Her dissertation focuses on the ways youth engage new media literacy practices with their peers as they navigate issues of college readiness and access.

Hui Soo Chae (contributor to Chapter 4) is a doctoral student whose dissertation focuses on using critical Asian theory to deconstruct master narratives of Korean American students in secondary schools.